TOWARDS SUSTAINABLE TOURISM

TOWARDS SUSTAINABLE TOURISM

Anand Bhallabh

AKANSHA PUBLISHING HOUSE
NEW DELHI - 110 002 (INDIA)

AKANSHA PUBLISHING HOUSE
4649/21-B, Ansari Road
Daryaganj, New Delhi - 110 002
Phones: 23263193, 9811582579, 9435116718
E-mail: ektabooks@yahoo.com

Towards Sustainable Tourism

First Published, 2007

ISBN 978-81-8370-123-5

PRINTED IN INDIA

Published by Akansha Publishing House, New Delhi - 110 002 and Printed at Capital Offset Press, Delhi

CONTENTS

PREFACE

> "Excessive ambitions necessarily entail great sacrifices. Much hoarding must be followed by heavy loss. He who knows when he has enough will not be put to shame."
>
> —*Lao Tzu*

> "We work day after day, not to finish things; but to make the future better.... because we will spend rest of our lives there."
>
> —*Charles F. Kettering*

No doubt, for overall development, tourism has contributed a lot. It is flourishing leaps and bound with bright prospects. Since most of the tourism resources are natural; overuse, misuse and abuse of these resources have caused severe damage to them. Simultaneously, tourism has great adverse impact on sociocultural environment of the destination countries/locations. Environmental degradation, imbalance of ecosystem, erosion/destruction of sociocultural values and gradual loss to heritage are some of the burning problems, caused by unplanned tourism activities.

Sustainable development and sustainable and ecotourism are the concepts which emerged to cope with the problem. More recently we hear and are witnessing global warming and climate change, which are much debated issues these days.

Keeping in view the severity of problem, prompt action must be taken to rectify the future course of tourism. William B. Given, Jr. has rightly said, "when possible make decision now, even if action is in the future. A reviewed decision usually is better than one reached at the last moment."

The present book is an effort in the direction of gathering fundamentals of sustainable tourism and allied issues. The information is analysed rationally and a unique synthesis is presented herein. The entire information is extracted from various authoritative sources—books, articles, monographs, research reports, abstracts etc. Every care is taken to reproduce factual information.

The following topics fall within the gamut of this work—Introduction; Sustainable Tourism Development; Basics of Sustainable Tourism Planning; Sustainable Tourism and International Action; and NGOs on Sustainable Tourism etc. Text of some important declarations, glossary and an exhaustive bibliography are added features of this book.

We express our gratitude to all those on whose views/ research findings, this volume is devised and developed. The real credit for this ought go to them. We are thankful to all those also who have provided all requisite material. We are grateful to our colleagues, friends and seniors who have inspired, guided and assisted us in many ways while working on this project. Last but not the least, we appreciate our publisher for evincing keen interest in publishing this book in superb way.

We will feel amply rewarded, if this effort could benefit the users—academically or professionally. Shortcomings, and constructive comments are welcome from all quarters to make it more informative and useful.

—AB

1

INTRODUCTION

> "The superior man thinks always of virtue; the common man thinks of comfort."
>
> —*Confucius*

Sustainable tourism, also known as responsible tourism, has been defined variously. Most tend to assume that all tourists are responsible for respecting and conserving a destination's economic, environmental, and socio-cultural balances.

Global economists forecast continuing international tourism growth, ranging between three and six percent annually, depending on the location. As one of the world's largest and fastest growing industries, this continuous growth will place great stress on remaining biodiverse habitats, often used to support mass tourism. Sustainable tourists are aware of these dangers and seek to protect their favorite destinations, and to protect tourism as an industry. Sustainable tourists face many responsibilities to reduce tourism's impact on communities, including:

- informing themselves of the culture, politics, and economy of the communities being visited.

- anticipating and respecting local cultures' expectations and assumptions.
- contributing to intercultural understanding and tolerance.
- supporting the integrity of local cultures by favoring businesses which conserve cultural heritage
- supporting local economies by purchasing local goods and participating with small, local businesses.
- conserving resources by seeking out businesses that are environmentally conscious, and by using the least possible amount of non-renewable resources.

The Multilateral Investment Fund (MIF) focus on destinations where there is already a critical mass of tourism businesses, MIF projects aim to boost the competitiveness of locally owned small and medium enterprises, helping them to organize themselves and work toward the shared goals of increasing income, employment and economic development and consequently social well-being..

Ecotourism

Heather Robinson (2006) says ecotourism, is a subset of sustainable tourism, differing by its focus on ecology. Ecotourism is sustainable tourism that "contributes actively to the conservation of natural and cultural heritage; includes local and indigenous communities in its planning, development and operation, contributing to their well-being; interprets the natural and cultural heritage of the destination to visitors; and lends itself better to independent travellers, as well as to organized tours for small size groups. In simple words ecotourism means while practicing any kind of tourism one should not harm nature. For today's fast changing world only the practice of ecotourism can save nature from ever growing human population. Ecotourism is the best way to practice any kind of tourism whether it is wildlife tourism, adventure tourism, or heritage tourism. It is the duty of all mankind to preserve nature and different species, only then can they survive for a long time; mankind should respect nature and its rules. Man should preserve nature for the upcoming generation, so they also feel the pleasure of being in nature as people of this and earlier generations felt.

Green Conventions

Alarmed by the degrading environmental conditions and their repercusion on life of all sorts on the earth, all nations and international organisations started pondering over the problem. As such as a recent development, Green conventions or green meetings are being conducted in ways which minimize the environmental burdens imposed by such activities. Green event planners apply environmentally preferred practices to waste management, resource and energy use, travel and local transportation, facilities selection, siting and construction, food provision and disposal, hotels and accommodations, and management and purchasing decisions.

Thus, Green event and convention planning is now an established trend within the global tourism and convention industry. Several cities in the United States and Europe now sport green convention centers designed using green building principles and practices. Many high visibility events including the Olympic Games in Italy, Sydney, Utah, and Greece; the World Summit on Sustainable Development in Johannesburg, and the 2004 Democratic and Republican National Conventions have implemented green practices with varied success. Such efforts aim to conserve resources, protect air and water quality, habitat and human health, and showcase sustainability practices and concerns.

Remarkably, parts of the tourism and convention industry now promote green meetings, conferences, and convention planning as demand for sustainability measures increases. Industry associations have produced standards and guides for green meetings. Government agencies and non-profit organizations also promote these practices with research, recommendations, grants and technical support. Some private consultants in the meeting planning industry specialize in mounting green events, and industry groups and governments now sponsor awards to recognize achievements in the concerned field.

Green conventions, meetings, conferencing and events are part of an international movement to achieve a sustainable world economy and livable planet.

Green Meeting Guides and Standards

- Environment Canada's Green Meeting Guide 2005
- Convention Industry Council's Green Meetings Report (English or German)
- Carbon Neutral Conferencing
- Green Globe 21: Benchmarking & Certification for Travel & Tourism
- Greenpeace Olympic Environmental Guidelines
- Sustainable Hotels Siting, Design and Construction

Government Agencies & Non-profit Organizations

- BlueGreen Meetings

- Ceres Green Hotel Initiative
- Coalition for Environmentally Responsible Conventions
- Green Globe 21
- Green Meetings Industry Council
- US Environmental Protection Agency: Green Meetings

Green Convention Centers

- Oregon Convention Center, Portland, OR
- Lawrence Convention Center, Pittsburgh, PA
- Greening Pittsburgh's Convention Center: Lessons in Market Transformation.

Large conventions, meetings and other major organized events drive the travel, tourism and hospitality industry. Cities and convention centers compete to attract such commerce, commerce which has heavy impacts on resource use and the environment. Major sporting events, such as the Olympic Games, present special problems regarding environmental burdens and degradation. But burdens imposed by the regular convention industry can be vastly more significant.

Green conventions and events are a new but growing sector and marketing point within the convention and hospitality industry. More environmentally aware organizations, corporations and government agencies are now seeking more sustainable event practices, greener hotels, restaurants and convention venues, and more energy efficient or climate neutral travel and ground transportation.

Additionally, some convention centers have begun to

take direct action in reducing the impact of the conventions they host. One example is the Moscone Center in San Francisco, California, which has a very aggressive recycling program, a large solar power system, and other programs aimed at reducing impact and increasing efficiency.

With the advent of the internet, some traditional conventions are being replaced with virtual conventions, where the attendees remain in their home physical location and "attend" the convention by use of a web-based interface programmed for the task. This sort of "virtual" meeting eliminates all of the impacts associated with travel, accommodation, food wastage, and other necessary impacts of traditional, physical conventions.

Sustainable Travel

Travel over long distances requires a large amount of either time or energy. Generally this involves burning fossil fuels, a largely unsustainable practice and one that contributes to climate change, via CO_2 emissions.

Air travel is perhaps the worst offender in this regard, contributing to between 2 and 3% of global carbon emissions. Given a business-as-usual approach, this could be expected to rise to 5% by 2015 and 10% by 2050. Car travel is the next worst offender.

Mass transport is the most climate friendly method of travel, and generally the rule is "the bigger the better" - compared to cars, buses are relatively more sustainable, and trains and ships are even more so. Human energy and renewable energy are the most efficient, and hence, sustainable. Travel by bicycle, solar powered car, or sailing boat produces no carbon emissions (although the embodied energy in these vehicles generally comes at the expense of carbon emission).

Sustainable Coastal Tourism

Many coastal areas are experiencing particular pressure from seachange growth in lifestyles and growing numbers of tourists. Coastal environments are limited in extent consisting of only a narrow strip along the edge of the ocean. Coastal areas are often the first environments to experience the detrimental impacts of tourism. Planning and management controls can reduce the impact on coastal environments and ensure that investment into tourism products supports sustainable coastal tourism.

Investment into appropriate coastal tourism infrastructure can also assist coastal environments support larger numbers of residents and tourists. Examples include paved esplanades that support large numbers of coastal visitors. The same number of visitors visiting an undeveloped coastline would feel much more crowded and damage sensitive coastal environments. Beach nourishment is an example of infratructure that supports the natural capacity of the environment [IENCE] to support tourist and resident lifestyles.

Sustainable Development

Sustainable development is defined as balancing the fulfillment of human needs with the protection of the natural environment so that these needs can be met not only in the present, but in the indefinite future. The linkage between environment and development was first made in 1980, when the International Union for the Conservation of Nature published the *World Conservation Strategy* and used the term "sustainable development." The concept came into general usage following publication of the 1987 report of the Brundtland Commission — formally, the World Commission on Environment and Development. Set up by the United Nations General Assembly, the Brundtland

Commission coined what was to become the most often-quoted definition of sustainable development as development that "meets the needs of the present without compromising the ability of future generations to meet their own needs."

The field of sustainable development can be conceptually broken into four constituent parts: environmental sustainability, economic sustainability, social sustainability and political sustainability.

Sustainable development does not focus solely on environmental issues. More broadly, sustainable development policies encompass three general policy areas: economic, environmental and social. In support of this, several United Nations texts, most recently the 2005 World Summit Outcome Document, refer to the "interdependent and mutually reinforcing pillars" of sustainable development as economic development, social development, and environmental protection.

The Universal Declaration on Cultural Diversity (UNESCO, 2001) elaborates further the concept by stating that "...cultural diversity is as necessary for humankind as biodiversity is for nature"; it becomes "one of the roots of development understood not simply in terms of economic growth, but also as a means to achieve a more satisfactory intellectual, emotional, moral and spiritual existence". In this vision, cultural diversity is the fourth policy area of sustainable development.

Green development is generally differentiated from Sustainable development in that Green development prioritizes what its proponents consider to be environmental sustainability over economic and cultural considerations. Proponents of Sustainable Development argue that it provides a context in which to improve overall sustainability where cutting edge Green development is unattainable. For example, a cutting edge treatment plant with extremely high maintenance costs may not be sustainable in regions of the world with less financial resources. An environmentally ideal plant that is shut down due to bankruptcy is obviously less sustainable than one that is maintainable by the indigenous community, even if it is somewhat less effective from an environmental standpoint.

Sustainable Development is an ambiguous concept, as a wide array of views has fallen under its umbrella. The concept has included notions of weak sustainability, strong sustainability and deep ecology. Different conceptions also reveal a strong tension between ecocentrism and anthropocentrism. Thus, the concept remains weakly defined and contains a large amount of debate as to its precise definition. During the last ten years, different organizations have tried to measure and monitor the proximity to what they consider sustainability by implementing what it has been called sustainability metric and indices.

Many environmentalists have criticized some interpertations of the term "sustainable development" as an oxymoron, claiming that economic policies based on concepts of growth and continued depletion of resources cannot be sustainable, since that term implies resources remain constant. Some people prefer the term "developing sustainability", as it does not imply that something needs to be created.

Environmental Sustainability

Environmental sustainability is defined as the ability of the environment to continue to function properly indefinitely. This involves meeting the present needs of humans without endangering the welfare of future generations. The goal of environmental sustainability is to minimize environmental degradation, and to halt and reverse the processes they lead to.

An "unsustainable situation" occurs when natural capital (the sum total of nature's resources) is used up faster than it can be replenished. Sustainability requires that human activity only uses nature's resources at a rate at which they can be replenished naturally. Theoretically, the long term result of environmental degradation would be local environments that are no longer able to sustain human populations to any degree. Such degradation on a global scale could imply extinction for humanity.

BACKPACKING

Rather a recent development, Backpacking is a term used to denote a form of low-cost independent international travel, differentiating it from other forms of tourism notably by the following typical attributes: minimal budget use, longer duration traveling, use of public transport and multiple destinations/countries. The origin of the name comes from the backpacks that budget travelers generally carry in the interests of mobility and flexibility.

Many commentators see backpacking as descriptive, not only of low-cost travel, but of the culture and philosophy often associated with it especially anti or trans-nationalism as well as a romanticization of wanderlust and a desire for "authentic" contact with local culture which in other forms of tourism may be spherical or less intensive.

Most probably, the term backpacking is originated in the early 1970s with the advent of low-cost jet airplane fares. During this era it became common for young Westerners, to follow the hippie trail into India and Southeast

Asia. This period also gave birth to the first budget guidebooks and began to change the way that many people looked at the possibilities and opportunities of travel.

More recently, backpacking has become something of a rite of passage in the popular culture of some countries, where after finishing high school, university or a period in the army they take several months to two years' break. Countries with geographic isolation such as Australia and New Zealand are such examples, but equally are the fact that like all countries that boast a high number of backpackers per capita they are affluent and English-speaking (or English as second language is common) countries where the majority of their citizens can afford overseas travel. Another typical example is the Netherlands. Likewise, a substantial amount of young adults from Israel also undertake long-term backpacking trips, particularly after they finish their mandatory military service. Travel of a backpacking nature is also extremely popular with Northern Europeans, particularly the Germans, Irish and British, and with Australians, Canadians, and New Zealanders.

Low-cost options are popular: such as sharing lifts, budget flights, rail/bus passes (or if the backpacking trip is circumglobal, a relatively cheap round-the-world air ticket which permits numerous stops), youth hostels, free hospitality services and buying food at supermarkets and sometimes cooking for oneself in kitchen equipped hostels abroad instead of going to restaurants.

Hostels and other budget accommodations in the 'developed' world tend to be communal to some degree, and thus backpacker culture is often highly social and emphasizes the camaraderie of communal life, such as the lounge area common in many hostels. When backpackers stay in one place for a while, they often seek a house-share with numerous other backpackers and are likely to share a room to keep the costs down.

The common language of backpackers is overwhelmingly English in varying levels of fluency. This is due to the fact that English is the first language of most from Commonwealth of Nations countries plus USA and Ireland. Another major reason for the popularity of English is that it is the most common second language of most Western Europeans.

Backpacker culture is perhaps typified by the Lonely Planet (Australian) series of guidebooks, which caters to budget travelers both in its regular guides as well as, more specifically, the "On a Shoestring" regional compilations. The Rough Guide (UK) and Let's Go (USA) series of guidebooks are also popular. In France, the traditional backpacker's guidebook is the *Guide du routard*.

Traditionally, backpackers do not travel with expensive electronic equipment such as laptop computers and PDAs due to concerns about theft, damage, and additional luggage weight. However, the desire to stay connected coupled with trends in lightweight electronics have given rise to the flashpacking trend.

The majority of backpackers are in their late teens and 20s. Patrons at most youth hostels are over 18 (some even mandate a minimum age of 18) while guests over 30 are more rare. The 'stereotypical' backpacker is often envisioned as a college student or recent graduate in their mid-twenties with no dependents (spouse, children), or permanent employment at home, therefore making it easier to put typical daily responsibilities on temporary hiatus to go traveling for months at a time. Depending on the part of the world, the median age of backpackers can vary. Australia, Europe, and North America generally appeal to more youthful travelers, while more 'difficult' regions such as South America or the Middle East attract older and more experienced travelers.

Rolf Potts writes in his book *Vagabonding* about what he sees as the myths that surround conventional travel:

Of all the outrageous throwaway lines one hears in movies, there is one that stands out for me. It doesn't come from a madcap comedy, an esoteric science-fiction flick, or a special-effects-laden action thriller. It comes from Oliver Stone's Wall Street, when the Charlie Sheen character — a promising big shot in the stock market — is telling his girlfriend about his dreams.

"I think if I can make a bundle of cash before I'm thirty and get out of this racket," he says, "I'll be able to ride my motorcycle across China."

When I first saw this scene on video a few years ago, I nearly fell out of my seat in astonishment. After all, Charlie Sheen or anyone else could work for eight months as a toilet cleaner and have enough money to ride a motorcycle across China. Even if they didn't yet have their own motorcycle, another couple months of scrubbing toilets would earn them enough to buy one when they got to China.

For many, this sums up the allure of backpacking, promising an "exotic" or "adventurous" experience that is also deemed "authentic," that is, an experience that, because it is self-planned and directed, does not fit within the typical Western-style vacation or travel industry.

This desire to experience "authentic" travel may be a reaction to the commercialization of the travel industry. Many backpackers express disdain towards "packaged" travel experiences including cruise ships and guided or bus tours which typically consist of a large number of tourists led by a guide. In contrast, backpacker philosophy encourages self-reliance and individuality, like overcoming the language barrier without the help of a translator or making all of one's own travel arrangements (to present two examples). John Gregory sums up this philosophy as:

Those spending big bucks for guided travel get peace-of-mind in return. They are guaranteed no worries, no hassles, an experience as close as possible to being home, without being home. They get an hour and fifteen minutes for the guaranteed-open museum, then a two-hour sightseeing ride that catches all the picture-postcard highlights. They break for lunch at a "recommended" restaurant, where the food is reasonable and ordering is easy. And as the next bus pulls in they re-board theirs to repeat the routine, ending with an easy check-in at a reasonable hotel, populated with plenty of other tourists, pretty much like themselves.

While all travel is good for the human spirit, budget backpacking is unparalleled for meeting people and experiencing worlds on their own intimate terms. There are many travelers who have the resources for pampered-class but choose to strap on a backpack and see the world via the seat-of-their-pants, because they know it's the best way to experience cultures and interact with local people.

In the United States among many other Western countries, this backlash against the large-scale commercial travel industry as expressed in the philosophy of backpacking has made some inroads into mainstream culture, such as in the popular travel guide writer Rick Steves who, like Tony and Maureen Wheeler of Lonely Planet, spun his experiences as a backpacker in the 1970s into a successful guidebook series.

In addition to notions of authenticity, some backpackers value the sense of freedom and independence in this mode of travel. Especially on extended trips, there is often only a rough itinerary, which can be changed at will. If a backpacker does not like a place, she can move on. If she likes it, she is free to stay and kick back for a while. Travel directions may change when a backpacker meets other independent travelers and learns about destinations she had not considered before or joins up with new friends. The semblance of "gypsy" life has its own romantic allure.

Of course, while backpack travel is carefree in this respect, it is more complicated in that backpackers have to plan everything and deal with all adversities themselves. There is no cruise director taking care of them. However, some backpackers also view this as a positive: It is a challenge and adventure, and the sometimes intense problem-solving in unfamiliar surroundings helps to hone their life skills.

Many long term backpackers gain temporary work (usually low-paid, unskilled, casual, and sometimes in violation of local labor laws) in the countries they visit. For instance, London's pubs are well known for the number of Australian bartenders working in them; "Irish pubs" around the world hire Irish backpackers. In Australia, fruit picking is a popular job among backpackers, although it can be physically demanding. Although while staying in one place for a long duration, say while working and living in semi-permanent accommodation it could be questioned whether you are still backpacking in the form of the adjective.

Backpackers are also commonly employed by hostels, where English-language proficiency and familiarity with hostel operations are considered assets. Hostels around the world are increasing their revenue by inaugurating work and travel programs, where hostelers can work for accommodation by performing basic hostel upkeep and operational duties.

Working backpackers are often facilitated through working holiday visas, commonly available to citizens under 30 of Commonwealth countries, Western Europe and Republic of Ireland.

Backpacker philosophy is sometimes criticized for being hypocritical. Some travelers have been known to forego finding "authentic" contact with a culture, and instead congregate only with other travelers in international hostels or guesthouses. Backpackers are accused of traveling to exotic places only to associate with other backpackers. Generally backpackers are from developed countries, speak very good or fluent English (even if haited from a non-English speaking country). When these backpackers arrive in developing countries they congregate at the hostels, guesthouses, bars in the center of town where they tend to not blend in.

Backpackers are sometimes blamed for the commercialization of the destinations they travel to. This can often lead to the overuse of certain natural and cultural resources or commercial exploitation of local people or the economy, a vice backpacking shares with other forms of tourism. A notable example of this phenomenon is Byron Bay in Australia, which was a largely quiet backpacker town in the 1970s and is now considered one of the most popular destinations in the 2000s with a bias for yuppies. This is sometimes said to actually pervert the backpacking culture itself: while backpackers seek genuineness and "authentic" cultural interactions, thus often looking for places with as few other foreigners as possible, they very often tend to meet in so-called "backpacker paradises" - places where all backpackers meet and that, eventually, end-up being modern-day "hippie-resorts". Examples include San Pedro de Atacama, a formerly isolated village in Chile and now a town dependent on tourism, and the island of Ko Pha Ngan in Thailand. This phenomenon is perhaps not unlike the phenomenon of gentrification that happens in urban ecologies.

A third layer of criticism is economic. Backpackers' pursuit of "cheap" travel destinations is only possible through the imbalance of living costs between Western and developing nations. Thus, backpacking can be seen as an inherently exploitative activity that benefits from the poverty of destination countries. South East Asia and much of Latin America are notable examples of very inexpensive countries which backpackers visit and have the ability to stay comfortably for months even on a relatively small budget. A more recent example includes the collapse of the peso currency in Argentina in the early 2000s, which quickly made that country a very attractive destination for budget backpackers.

Another criticism is a perception of language arrogance by many backpackers, particularly those from largely monolingual English-speaking countries such as Australia or the USA. While having a common language is a defining feature of backpacking, monolingual backpackers (who overwhelmingly speak English) are sometimes accused of being too arrogant with their use of English while abroad.

A common citation is the assumption that youthful people and those working in the tourism industry in many countries around the world are now proficient in English or that English-speaking help will not be difficult to find, as opposed to learning and speaking the local language at even just a basic level out of self-interest or respect.

Finally, one more layer of criticism is the impact a heavy flow of backpackers can have on local cultures, especially in developping countries. The presence of large numbers of people who do not respect local customs can have effects that range from being a mild irritant to locals to being damageable to the local culture's long-term integrity. For example, a significant number of backpackers take their cues from each other and engage in behaviours that are not acceptable to their host country (such as dressing inappropriately, sunbathing topless or engaging in public displays of affection), despite the multiple warnings in guidebooks. Besides creating animosity against backpackers, this has led to some backpacking beach communities to become local attractions for young local men (such as many beaches in India). Also damaging is the heavy use of drugs, alcohol and tobacco made by some backpackers. For many, these habits are not representative of their habits at home. However, many youth in the host country are constantly exposed to backpackers displaying these behaviours. This can encourage them to adopt similar behaviours.

Benefits

In their defense, some backpackers say that budget travel pumps money into the economies of Third World countries, increasing their standard of living and creating jobs, and doing this in a way that is inherently more egalitarian than mainstream tour companies, who often operate with minimal contact with third party vendors or average citizens. Backpacking in comparison, frequently makes use of local food vendors, merchants and accommodations, and thus does more to benefit the local economy. The lower cost to the budget-conscious young Western tourist and the increased patronage to local merchants can actually make the economics of backpacking a win-win situation in many cases.

Destinations

It is worth noting that there is a notable difference between backpacking travel in the developed world, typically Australia, New Zealand, North America and Europe where hostels are commonly used, than in the developing world, typically South and South-East Asia, Africa and Latin America. In such developing nations travel is cheaper, but often harder. Equally where backpacking is popular, whole industries have established to tend to the needs of backpackers offering services (often in English) to make their travel easier (laundry, visa applications, "backpacker" tours, budget travel booking services). Plus bars/restaurants showing sporting events from 'back home' and bootleg copies of movies. Well known examples of such places would be the Khaosan Road in Bangkok, Anjuna in Goa and Antigua Guatemala in Guatemala. In backpacker hot-spots, many bars and restaurants are set up primarily for backpackers with few locals patronizing them - this again fosters the social aspect of backpacking travel.

Classically, Western Europe is a very common backpacker destination because of the availability of public transport and intercity transport and the large number of hostels and other budget accommodations, not to mention the immense sense of history and culture which permeates from this region. However, since the fall of the Berlin Wall, Eastern Europe has become a rapidly growing destination for budget travelers. Originally this meant cities such as Prague and Budapest, but more recently Poland, Slovenia, Croatia, the Balkans, and the Baltic Republics have become a popular stops on the backpacking circuit.

Long-term backpacker destinations are places in the developing world with low costs of living such as Goa (India), Essaouira (Morocco), or Thailand. Australia's East Coast, which is also colloquially known as the 'Goon Trail', is also a very popular destination for many backpackers, and particularly for those who enjoy non-stop beaches and party atmospheres.

Evidently, as mentioned above, certain destinations are so popular on the backpacking circuit that some cities house "backpacker ghettos," whole districts where large numbers of travellers congregate to find cheap accommodation, street food, and share travel information. The most famous of these is the Khaosan Road area of downtown Bangkok.

Remarkably, most backpacking follows established routes with terms such as the 'gringo trail' in Latin America and the 'Banana Pancake' or trail' in Southeast Asia used. These routes and popular countries generally focus on three factors. And finally round the world air travel routing and airline hubs.

Thailand is a very popular backpacker destination and is an obvious stop-off between Europe and Australia with Bangkok Airport a major Asian hub. Consider the Philippines which has no overland connections, is not a major stop-off and holds slightly similar attributes to Thailand. The same is true of Eastern Europe's and Central America's proximity to affluent Western Europe and North America.

While largely a matter of nationality, personal taste and the current political situation, some generalizations can be made about the destinations many backpackers avoid. For example, a fair number of backpackers, like many other tourists, avoid countries where there is a perceived danger of terrorism, kidnapping, hijacking, food poisoning or hassle in the way of getting a visa or repeatedly being accosted to purchase goods/services. Some countries have tried to address these issues or unfair perceptions. Morocco, which at some point had one of the worst reputations in this regard, is reported to have clamped down on hustling and touting aimed at foreign travellers.

In Asia and Eastern Europe, visa regulations are being greatly relaxed encourage more travellers, especially as many Eastern European nations have now joined the European Union. In Egypt, Turkey and Pakistan huge efforts are made to safeguard travelers from terrorism and countries such as Syria and Iran, while holding terrible reputations abroad are welcoming of backpackers (once issued with a visa).

High Costs

Regions with a high cost of living, such as Scandinavia for example, are avoided by many long-term backpackers because of the expense. Other destinations which have high costs for transportation, such as Polynesia or Alaska are also avoided by the majority of backpackers.

This applies to a lesser degree to many destinations in Western Europe, where costs are generally high enough to discourage extensive (three months and longer) budget travel, particularly when the Euro is trading very strong. The advent of low cost airlines in Europe have assisted in keeping transportation costs down. Travel to popular but extremely expensive cities such as New York City, Tokyo or London is generally limited to just several days.

Good infrastructure, especitally easy accessibility is prefered by the back porkers. While not an absolute, countries without developed infrastructure, especially in the form of public transportation, are more difficult for backpackers to travel in because of the serious limits on mobility. This includes many African countries and the greater part of Central Asia.

Hostels in the United States are also generally expensive in comparison to many other countries, often at least $US20-30 per person per night especially in the large cities. The prevalence of motel chains, catering primarily to private motorists, may contribute to the relatively small number of backpacker hostels in the USA.

A further constraint for backpackers in the United States is that they have few, if any, options to partake in legitimate employment. This is in contrast to the vast array of reciprocal working holiday arrangements which are in place with most of the Commonwealth of Nations and Western European countries.

While the desire to travel at low cost and the desire to travel with convenience and security are often at odds, some countries are generally avoided by backpackers because of the general political instability. In the most extreme cases, such as Iraq, Somalia or North Korea opportunities for travel may be severely curtailed or an outright impossibility. Other areas are avoided by many backpackers because of the perceived general hostility of the political climate, including some parts of the Middle East and Central Asia, Indonesia and parts of Central Africa and Latin America.

Some countries are largely avoided by backpackers due to a substantially increased risk of being kidnapped or mugged of their possessions, to the point where the benefits of travel may not compensate for their dangers. Colombia in South America is a notable example, which has the unfortunate reputation of having one of the highest number of kidnappings per capita in the world. Many other South American cities, such as Rio de Janeiro, São Paulo and Lima, also have high crime rates. Moreover, African cities such as Johannesburg or Nairobi are also discouraged on the backpacker circuit due to their high crime rates and perceived danger of visiting.

Health is another issue of concern for backpackers with sometimes poor health facilities away from urban hubs and prevalence of diseases such as in some regions, malaria and yellow fever. This is particular the case in developing South East Asia and most of Africa. More common, however are minor ailments like sunburn, diarrhoea or food poisoning, which seems to be an unfortunate caveat of third world travel. This includes women's health issues such as the availability of tampons or prescription medications like the birth control pill.

Many backpackers try to avoid crowds of other (ordinary) tourists. Such places may also be undesirable because of high costs, inauthentic culture, limited sightseeing options and exclusively prebooked accommodation. This may include exclusive resort islands such as those in the Caribbean.

Language Barriers

While a matter of personal taste, willingness to learn foreign languages, and other stipulations, countries where the English language is not widely understood or holds little sway in everyday life can be seen as a hindrance for independent travel for those who do not speak the local language. This tends to include destinations in the developing world where English is not commonly spoken such as Latin America, many parts of Africa, Central Asia, and more rural areas of East Asia, the Middle East, Russia and other parts of the former Soviet Union. However, this can also be seen as challenging, so it can also draw many backpackers to these regions as "off the beaten track" locations.

NEO TOURISM

As a new coinage the term Neo Tourism is pioneered by the Korea Tourism Organization that comprehensively describes the newly changing trend of the tourism.

Following the changes in the economic, social and cultural paradigm of the 20th century, the form of tourism is changing as well. "Neo Tourism" is a term that comprehensively describes the new aspects of such changes and diversification of the tourism. The "Neo Tourism" incorporates concepts such as 'Sustainable tourism' which puts emphasis on the environmental sustainability and 'Special Interest Tourism (SIT)' which reflects postmodern social phenomenon.

Infact, initially the term "Neo Tourism" was generated to explain a form of tourism which has not existed before, to say, "New Tourism". However, with continuous advents of various types of tourism, it has become necessary to categorize those concepts in further details and eventually the "Neo Tourism" has taken more concrete meaning as such including the essential key words in the category. Those essential key words are as follows.

(a) Postmodernism

(b) Sustainability

(c) Digitalization

It is significant to note that the term "Neo Tourism" can explain the following types of tourism.

(i) Tourism that satisfies individual interests and purposes appearing with post-modern social change.
(ii) Tourism that avoids the environmental destruction and ensure experiencing the untouched nature.
(iii) Tourism that manages various matters such as gathering information and making reservation through Internet.

Remarkably, "Neo Tourism" can be used from the suppliers' point of view as well as the customers' in the following concepts.

(a) Utilizing IT technology such as internet and ubiquitous systems to promote and sale the tourism products.
(b) Developing environmentally and socially sustainable tourist attractions.
(c) Creating a new type of tourism product by connecting tourism industry with other industries. (ex. Medical tourism, Edu Tourism).

MAJOR EVENTS

Some of the landmarks on the sustainable tourism are furnished below:

1. 1972— UN Conference on the Human Environment, Stockholm.
2. 1980— Manila Declaration on World Tourism.
3. 1987— The Report, 'Our Common Future'.
4. 1992— The Rio Declaration and the Adoption of Agenda 21.

5. 1996— Adoption of Agenda 21 for Travel and Tourism industry.
6. 1997— Male Declaration on Sustainable Tourism development; Manila Declaration on the Social Impact of Tourism; Resolution of the 19th Special session of the UN General Assembly Requesting the Commission on Sustainable Development to develop an Action oriented international programme of work on sustainable tourism in coordination with the WTO, UNEP and other UN agencies.
7. 1998— Resolution of the UN General Assembly proclaiming 2002 as the International Year of Ecotourism as well as the International Year of the Mountains.
8. 1999— WTO General Assembly accepts the Global Code of Ethics; The UN Commission on Sustainable Development takes note of the Global Code of Ethics and expresses interest in it.
9. 2001— UN General Assembly adopts resolution emphasizing the importance of responsible and sustainable tourism and takes note of the Global Code of Ethics with interest.
10. 2002— World Summit on Ecotourism.
11. 2002— World Summit on Sustainable Development.

Obviously the developments so far highlight two major trends. First, the WTO has been consistently pursuing the importance of sustainable tourism and its relevance within the wider concept of sustainable development. In fact the Manila Declaration of 1980 can be termed as the pathfinder on the subject, much before the world had taken serious note of the importance of the concept of sustainability. Second, unfortunately the pioneering initiatives of the WTO remained largely confined to the tourism sector only.

Till 1997 the issue of sustainable tourism was not seriously discussed in the UN system. The Commission on Sustainable Development discussed this subject only in relation to the small developing island states. Even the much lauded Rio declaration was heavily environment focussed and did not mention tourism as such. Agenda 21 did take tourism into account but not in an integrated manner. The UN General Assembly in its 19th Special Session, while reviewing the progress of implementation of Agenda 21, however, acknowledged the importance of tourism and placed tourism in the agenda of the Commission. The commission in its seventh session in 1999 organised a multi-stakeholders' dialogue on sustainable tourism and accorded the status of an economic sector to tourism. One significant decision of this Commission was to draw up an international work programme on sustainable tourism, a decision WTO should be closely associated within implementation. It is well recognised that travel and tourism promote awareness about environmental issues. A well-managed tourism can add substantially to environmental sustainability. And tourism itself requires a high quality environment and eco–system for its sustenance. Many tourism destinations flourish only because of the quality of their environment. Though tourism arrivals increased ten fold between 1970 and 2000, in the early 80s the negative effects of tourism had not yet shown too strongly. The primary concern those days were for the environment and ecology, and tourism was not seen as a great spoiler. Moreover, tourism is a complex, multi-dimensional multi-sectoral activity. While the generic term tourism might have escaped the attention of those who were planning for sustainable development, it is possible that many of the components of tourism were adequately addressed in these initiatives.

Sustainable development covers so many diverse aspects within its fold that any attempt to define it must risk the danger of either stating too much or too little. However the principles enunciated in the Brundtland Commission's report remains till today the most comprehensive exposition of the concept. It defines sustainable development as "development that meets the needs of the present without compromising the ability of future generations to meet their own needs." Further it says, "In essence, sustainable development is a process of change in which the exploitation of resources, the direction of investments, the orientation of technological development, and institutional change are all in harmony and enhance both current and future potential to meet human needs and aspirations." This basic principle has been further elaborated in the Earth Summit in Rio in 1992. Agenda 21 gave shape to these objectives by drawing up an exhaustive action programme.

The objective of sustainable development should be, it is argued, to enable each generation to enrich the inheritance. Use of resources should not be seen in too restrictive a sense. The development process involves use of resources. Stability of resources should be maintained in some aggregate macro sense and need not necessarily be too restrictive in every use in every place. Sustainable development, it is said, should go beyond the concern for the physical to societal and cultural values. The thrust of 'our common future' it was felt, did not adequately reflect the pressing concerns of poverty and economic sustainability.

The WTO attempted a definition of the concept of sustainable tourism way back in 1988. As it followed the report of the Brundtland Commission, it did have the influence of the wider definition on sustainable development. "Sustainable tourism development", it says, "meets the needs of present tourists and host regions while protecting and enhancing opportunity for the future. It is envisaged as leading to management of all resources in such a way that economic, social, and aesthetic needs can be fulfilled while maintaining cultural integrity, essential ecological processes, biological diversity, and life support systems."

The most pressing problem of sustainable development in the world today has been tardy implementation. The ideas need wider acceptability and understanding, particularly at the grass-roots level where philosophical debates and ideology pale in relation to hard realities. The first basic requirement is to frame the concept and action agenda in terms understandable to the targeted society and related to their environment and ethos.

As the world prepares to review the progress of action ten years after Rio, there is candid admission that despite domestic and international actions there is still a major gap in the implementation of Agenda 21.

Papers of the preparatory committee for the World summit recognize this gap. The Summit will have to chart out the strategy for the future on the basis of the shared experience of the past. The background papers for the Summit recognize the need to "promote sustainable tourism development in order to increase benefits from tourism resources for the population in the host communities, and maintain the cultural and environmental integrity of the host communities."

In the 198 action points drawn up there are many in which tourism can directly or indirectly contribute but the role of tourism has been specified only in relation to the Small Island Developing States. Naturally, as in the past the primary concern is with the physical environment. Many questions need to be asked if one wants to frame a strategy for the future.The need for sustainable development is universally accepted. Yet why do unsustainable practices come about? Why do those who are to implement sustainable practices sometimes meet failures? Are they unwilling or incapable? It is necessary to look at underlying causes rather than the symptoms. Policies are most effective when they look at the root causes.

For a long time beneath the general acceptance of the concept there was simmering difference, if not conflict, in vision among the developed and the developing and underdeveloped nations. Many activists saw the growing concern for sustainable development as the rich countries' self interest and attempt to take away attention from the pressing problems of hunger, poverty, malnutrition and so on. For example, the Second Citizen's Report on the State of India's Environment in 1985-86 had clearly voiced this apprehension. "One lesson is" it says, "therefore clear: the main cause of environmental destruction in the world is the demand for natural resources generated by the consumption of the rich...". In the 1972 UN conference such views were strongly aired. The Brazilian delegation had said "smoke is a sign of progress". And India's Prime Minister Mrs. Gandhi's statement—"poverty is the biggest polluter" was quoted again and again. Since 1972 things have changed.

The World Development Report of 1992, for example, categorically states that there is strong evidence of links between poverty alleviation and sustainable goals. The World Summit in Rio recognised this imperative and Principle 5 of the declaration regards "eradication of poverty as an indispensable requirement for sustainable development". Agenda 21 logically identifies many action points for poverty alleviation as part of sustainable development strategy. However by now it is recognised that independent action on poverty falls short of the desired effect. As early as 1984 the UNEP in a report had pointed out the adverse effects of heavy debt burden and adverse terms of trade on the environment of the Third World. There is growing realisation that the strategy for sustainable development must be based on an integrated socio-economic planning. The 7th meeting of the Commission on Sustainable Development in 1999 emphasized the need to link sustainable development to an integrated strategy for poverty reduction. It urged governments to "maximise the potential of tourism for eradication of poverty by developing appropriate strategies in co-operation with all major groups, indigenous and local communities." As noted earlier, the World Summit later this year does not seem to be working on the same perception of a role for tourism in the integrated economic development strategy for poverty eradication. This is an area which the tourism community and the WTO could push with vigour. Analysis of tourism data shows that in most countries with high levels of poverty, tourism has a significant contribution to the GDP and has potential of substantial further growth. This development may have two implications—the happy one that tourism is becoming the change agent for economic development; or the unhappy possibility that in this quest of using tourism as a tool for development , sustainable concerns can be relegated to the background. There is greater need therefore, of integrating the sustainable tourism initiatives to the overall sustainable development strategies.

Infact, both the Travel and Tourism Agenda 21 and the Global Code of Ethics are refreshingly focussed, clear and brief. Even then they gain more acceptability and become easier to implement if the WTO succeeds in integrating them to the general agenda of action.

In the same vein, quite often sectoral and rigid approach of the stakeholder groups cannot only create difficulties in implementation of the agenda but also can defeat the very objectives. One can mention the experience in Andaman and Nicobar Islands in India. A comprehensive tourism development plan for the island was drawn up with the assistance of the WTO and UNDP.

However the project had to satisfy very detailed scrutiny of the environment agencies which took time . In the meantime environmental degradation for expanding tourism, which was not properly planned and regulated, went on. The dilemma was that while there was no check on unsustainable activities by private persons, the tourism department's intention of planning sustainable development stumbled at the rigid interpretations of sustainable norms. Implementation also has not been satisfactory because in most cases yardsticks for assessing implementation are deficient or lacking. In most cases there is no accountability for non-implementation. The WTO has done pioneering work by developing a set of guidelines for local planners and for monitoring various sustainable tourism norms. The next step is to motivate the national governments to accept these guidelines and use them extensively and to build in some form of accountability at every stage for non-performance.

The Rio Declaration has 27 principles and the thrust of the principles are—

1. Human beings are at the centre of concern for sustainable development.
2. The right to development must be fulfilled so as to equitably meet environmental and development needs of present and future generations.
3. Environmental protection should be seen as integral part of development and not in isolation.
4. Eradication of poverty is an integral part of the requirement.
5. Global partnership is needed.
6. Public awareness and participation are important elements of the strategy.
7. Effective environmental legislations should be put in place.
8. Indigenous people and local communities should have a vital role in the implementation of sustainable development strategies.

Agenda 21 followed as a detailed comprehensive plan of action grouped into 40 chapters and more than 100 separate action areas. This wide ranging programme of action was adopted by the 182 countries that participated in the Conference.

The Travel and Tourism Agenda 21 (TT Agenda 21) identifies three core tools which can be used for achieving the objectives—

(a) regulations;

(b) free market mechanism;

(c) industry-led voluntary programmes.

Thus, the TT Agenda itself points out that regulations

should play only a supportive role. Over regulation often confuses the issues, and often become ineffective unless there is a strong and efficient mechanism for monitoring their implementation. One of the grievances expressed in the Second Citizens Report on the State of the Environment in India was that there was "too much of a policeman's attitude" in managing sustainable development.

More than 200 central and state laws existed at that time. This was not proportionate to the benefits derived from them. The TT Agenda itself calls the other two proposed tools unusual. It refers to some good examples of the market delivering the desired objectives. The Secretary General of WTO in his address to the second Tourism Summit in Geneva in 2000 had indicated how the market can work. The market chooses the desirable.

Lamentably, the developing and underdeveloped countries suffer from many market imperfections. Leaving sustainable management to the market may, it is feared in some cases aggravate the malady. As is often said in the developing countries, use of such measures must be tempered with a human face. In fact the background paper on the Local authority perspective prepared for the Seventh session of the Commission on sustainable Development in 1999 states the fear more strongly—"...the primary barrier to sustainable development through tourism is an over reliance on market mechanisms to guide tourism development and consumption decisions. The market...is insensitive to many requirements of sustainable tourism." In particular, reliance on the market may be disadvantageous to the poor countries and can work as an indirect trade barrier.

The UN General Assembly, in its resolution on tourism in the 19th Special Session, had advised the Commission on Sustainable Development to look at tourism as one of the largest industries and fastest growing economic sectors. The key areas of action identified in the resolution are—

1. Develop an action oriented international programme of work on sustainable tourism;
2. Develop shared interest of all the stakeholders;
3. Pay special attention to the relationship between environmental protection and conservation and sustainable tourism;
4. Strengthen national policy development and enhance capacity in the areas of physical planning, monitoring, use of regulatory mechanisms, information, education and marketing;
5. Assistance of the international community including the international financial institutions in achieving the above objectives.

The Secretary General of the WTO in his address to the World Tourism Summit in Geneva in 2000 had stressed—"today sustainable development is seen as a necessary concern; tomorrow it will be an inescapable requirement." The problem with tomorrow is that it never comes and we can always be moving into that inevitable calamity in a relaxed anticipation devoid of urgency. The tomorrow is almost on us and we have to face the realities.

To quote the Secretary General again—"the concept of sustainable development is global by definition. The 'future' is inevitably 'common'. It has been pointed out that world peace, sustainable development, world market for goods and services are examples of international public goods. They will be under provided without conscious, collective and concerted action.

All the reports and resolutions of the UN and other related organisations that we have examined have strongly urged for international initiatives on sustainable tourism involving all the UN agencies. This co-ordination mechanism has to be formalised and put in place.

To prevent wastage of efforts and resources, as well as to avoid duplication, integration of the action plans to the extent possible should be attempted. Sustainable tourism projects succeeds more if they are not in isolation. A case study of sustainable city—tourism in Heidelberg has established that—

(a) Only the integration of the activities for a sustainable tourism into an overall city concept e.g. the local Agenda 21 or a city development plan, can produce visible success;

(b) Isolated measures to the sole benefit of tourism are not accepted by the population. The most important features are the networked projects.

International Funding for Sustainable Tourism

There is unanimity among all agencies on the importance of international financing institutions playing a specific and important role in furthering sustainable development initiatives. The UN General Assembly Resolution 44/228 of 1989 is categorical on the subject. It directs the UN Conference on Environment and development to (a) identify ways and means of new and additional financial resources, (b) quantify financial requirements, (c) identify means of supporting developing countries in their efforts for sustainable developments. Agenda 21 has clearly spelt out the dimensions of the steps to be taken.

Now that the UN has clearly accepted tourism as an

important economic sector contributing to poverty eradication and environmental preservation, the WTO should make concrete its sustainable development plans for additional international financing in two stages. The first is for its own international integrated initiatives involving all their tourist sector interest groups. The second is to help performing nations to expand their sustainable tourism activities. By financially encouraging good work of some countries the WTO will be able to inspire the others. In all cases of direct financing of projects by international financial institutions, can the agreement also include a clause that a few key parameters of sustainable tourism would be implemented by the receiving country?

The problems of sustainable tourism can be seen from two angles—supply and demand. On the demand side most of the unsustainable behaviour of the tourists arise from either ignorance of the local customs and norms or from what is called the 'away from home syndrome'. In either case the need is for creating awareness and education. On the supply side the major problem in most developing countries is what is termed as the 'irridex' effect—the irritation caused to the local population because of diversion of services in short supply for the use of the tourists. There is also the potent problem of overuse of the physical and non-renewable resources for economic gains from tourism. In many cases action is wanting either for ignorance or lack of capability.

Action to counter these trends has to be sharp focussed. In the developing countries, it will be primarily to build capacity and enhance competence. The developed countries produce the largest outbound tourists. Education, awareness and preventive steps should start in these countries as well.

The long quest for sustainable development has aroused global interest in the future of man's journey in this planet. It has brought together the international community to deliberate on a common strategy of development for our common future. Much has been achieved but much more remains to be done.

2

SUSTAINABLE TOURISM DEVELOPMENT

> "Our most valuable possessions are those which can be shared without lessening — those which, when shared, multiply. Our least valuable possessions, on the other hand, are those which, when divided, are diminished."
>
> —*William H. Danforth*

For elucidating the importance of sustainble tourism, it is pertinent to reproduce an episode from the USA, which expresses the love and attachment for nature inherent in Red Indians.

In 1855, US President Franklin Pierce made a 'request' to Chief Sealth of the Suwanish tribe of American Indians, who live in what is now the State of Washington, to 'sell' his land to the Government. In reply, Chief Sealth sent the following letter to the President: "How can you buy or sell the sky, the warmth of the land? The idea is strange to us. Yet we do not own the freshness of the air or the sparkle of the water. How can you buy them from us? Every part of this earth is sacred to my people. Every shining pine needle, every sandy shore, every mist in the dark woods, every clearing and humming insect is holy in the memory and experience of my people..." "...And what is there to life if a man cannot hear the lovely cry of the whippoorwill or the argument of the frogs around a pond at night? The Red Indian prefers the soft sound of the wind itself cleaned by the midnight rain, or scented with a pine. The air is precious to the Red man, for all things share the same breath—the beasts, the trees, the man. The White man does not seem to notice the air he breathes. Like a man dying for many years, he is numbed to the smell... When the last Red man has vanished from the earth, and the memory is only the shadow of a cloud moving across the prairie, these shores and forests will still hold the spirits of my people."

The World Commission on Environment and Development CWCED defines 'sustainable development' as "development that meets the needs of the present without compromising the ability of future generations to meet their own needs". Since the 1992 Earth Summit, the concept of 'sustainable development' has been placed firmly on the global agenda and this issue is assuming great significance in the development of tourism. There are basically three principles of sustainable development. These principles are equally applicable to tourism development as well. Firstly, development must be ecologically sustainable, i.e., the ecological processes must not be adversely affected. Secondly, social and cultural sustainability — which means that tourism development is compatible with the culture and values of the local people and that the basic cultural identity of the community is not adversely affected. Thirdly, development must be economically sustainable in a process which allows such development to take place in an efficient management of resources. Such management must ensure that the resources can support the future as well as the current generations. Unfortunately, quite often, the negative aspects of tourism development get highlighted whereas the benefits which flow directly or indirectly are not noticed. The WTO Publication entilled—'*Sustainable Tourism Development: Guide for Local Planners* has summed up a model form of sustainable tourism as one designed to —

- improve the quality of life of the people;
- provide a good experience to the tourists; and
- maintain the quality of environment which is essential for both the tourists and local community.

Further more, benefits of sustainable tourism has been summed up very adequately as follows:

- "Sustainable tourism encourages an understanding of the impacts of tourism on the natural, cultural, and human environments.
- Sustainable tourism ensures a fair distribution of benefits and costs.
- Tourism generates local employment, both directly in the tourism sector and in various support and resource management sectors.
- Tourism stimulates profitable domestic industries—hotels and other lodging facilities, restaurants and other food services, transportation systems, handicrafts, and guide services.
- Tourism generates foreign exchange for the country and injects capital and the new money into the local economy.
- Tourism diversifies the local economy, particularly in rural areas where agricultural employment may be sporadic or insufficient.

- Sustainable tourism seeks decision-making among all segments of the society, including local populations, so that tourism and other resource users can coexist. It incorporates planning and zoning which ensure tourism development appropriate to the carrying capacity of the ecosytem.
- Tourism stimulates improvements to local transportation, communications, and other basic community infrastructures.
- Tourism creates recreational facilities which can be used by local communities as well as domestic and international visitors. It also encourages and helps pay for preservation of archaeological sites, and historic buildings and districts.
- Nature tourism encourages productive use of lands which are marginal for agriculture, enabling large tracts to remain covered in natural vegetation.
- Cultural tourism enhances local community esteemand provides the opportunity for greater understanding and communication among peoples of diverse backgrounds.
- Environmentally sustainable tourism demonstrates the importance of natural and cultural resources to a community's economic and social well-being and can help to preserve them.
- Sustainable tourism monitors, assesses and manages the impacts of tourism, develops reliable methods of environmental accountability, and counters any negative effect."

The inter-relation between the benefits of sustainable tourism, the responsibility of the Government and the local community is demonstrated in the following illustration.

Tourists

- Generate income through spending on transportation, food, lodging, etc.
- Wages, taxes,
- Foreign exchange.

Benefits

- Cultural experience & interaction
- Better understanding
- Unique experience

Government Sustainable Tourism

- Policies
- Standards
- Incentives
- Protect heritage, nature, wildlife
- Encourage cultural preservation

Community Benefits

- Employment
- Income
- Cultural interaction
- Better infrastructure
- Patronage of art/craft culture

Provide

- Visitor services and experience

- Participation in protection and development of local products
- Cultural interaction.

(McIntyre)

It is obvious that in any sustainable tourism planning, the environment, the ecology and the community are the key considerations. In planning sustainable tourism, therefore, an awareness about what is commonly referred to as the carrying capacity is of fundamental importance. Carrying capacity which covers ecological relationship, socio-cultural impact, and visitor experience cannot always be adequately quantified but nevertheless an understanding of the same is of importance. Carrying capacity basically refers to an assessment of the maximum use of any tourism site which does not cause tension for the host community and avoids adverse impact on the resources and on the psychological satisfaction of the tourists. Conflicts, however, are inherent in the very process of tourism development.

The issues which may cause such tensions have been beautifully examined in the background paper "The Social Impacts of Tourism" prepared by Professor C.L. Jenkins for the World Tourism Leaders Meeting on Social Impacts of Tourism in Manila, Philippines on 22nd May, 1997 For the tour operators and travel agents who sell the tourism products, it is primarily a commercial proposition. There is, therefore, an inherent potential of conflict between what sells and what the Government and local agencies would like to project. Prof. Jenkins also refers to cultural stress caused by what is called 'demonstration effect". Such effect results from transferring to the host community, examples and experiences of different cultures and lifestyles and also of different income levels which brings a sense of exploitation to the local community. But Prof. Jenkins has shown that cultural deterioration need not be caused by tourism development alone and not even by tourism development primarily. Such changes are influenced by many factors including economic factors. To what extent a society can insulate itself against such deterioration will depend on the awareness generated in the community, the Government policy towards protection and the willingness of those who are affected to take steps for such protection, and also on the inherent strength of the social fabric itself.

An adverse impact of tourism could also be in relation to the stress that the local systems have to undergo as a result of the large inflow of the tourists. Unless tourism is properly and carefully planned, greater pressure from visitors can cause what is called *"irridex effect"* — causing irritation to the local people because they are deprived of the basic civic amenities which are diverted for the benefit of the tourists. Tourism growth may change the rhythm of a community's lifestyle. In most cases, all such effects are possible but they need not necessarily be present in all cases. Quite often, such tension arises out of a tourist's lack of knowledge of the local culture and tradition and the weakness of the local system in handling the same. The agenda for action, therefore, should concentrate around community participation in tourism development and planning, training of the personnel associated with tourism development so that they can provide quality services without devaluing the same. In the framework of action it is necessary to ensure that the benefits to the community are so spread out that the people perceive the benefits flowing to them. Similarly, there is need for a legal and procedural framework that deals adequately with social evils like exploitation, child abuse, sex tourism, interference with heritage products, etc. Tourism can provide immense benefits and an be a tool for protection and preservation of the heritage of the country.

Instead of being seen as an irritant to sustainable development, a little initiative from the planners can make tourism the vehicle for preservation of ecology and heritage. Harping on the negative aspect only could be self-defeating academic dogmatism not in tune with the future aspirations and requirements of mankind. The National Tourism Policy, 1982 emphasised the importance of a judicious balance between conservation and development. "A major consideration of tourism development," the Policy states, "will be to preserve our culture and natural heritage which constitutes the major tourism resource of the country". Since then, however, major changes have taken place in the socio-economic and political situation in India and the global geo-political realities have also undergone tremendous changes. The country is now launching its Ninth Five Year Plan. In the beginning of this decade, India also embarked on a major policy of economic reforms and liberalisation and moved away from the rigours of quantitative controls of planned economic development to a liberalised, reformed and market-driven economic regime. In the changed scenario, the Government is having a new look at the Tourism Policy. The published draft of the new policy has—

(i) placed tourism as a central input in the economic development process because of its role in resource generation and employment creation;

(ii) focussedon the role of tourism in socio-economic development of the backward areas, weaker sections, women and artisans;

(iii) allowed these goals to be pursued in tune with the goal of the enrichment of the environment and the ecosystem; and

(iv) recognised the role of tourism as a potent global force for national and international understanding and for creating awareness for sustainable development.

Any policy for sustainable development will naturally revolve around the following cardinal principles,—

(a) that there is need for striking a balance between development and conservation;

(b) that there is need for commitment of the nation as a whole to the goals of sustainable tourism development;

(c) that adequate, effective and pragmatic control systems are devised and are efficiently put into place; and

(d) that the policy incorporates and motivates cooperation of the local community who must perceive the benefit of such participation and should be able to partake the same.

India is fortunate and unique in having such geographical diversity that has given it a wealth of ecosystems which are well protected and preserved. These ecosystems have become the major resources for eco-tourism in India. These consist of:

- biosphere reserves;
- mangroves;
- corals and coral reefs;
- deserts;
- mountains and forests;
- flora and fauna; and
- sea, lakes and rivers.

The policy objectives mentioned above particularly in the context of ecotourism can be achieved only by a process of selective approach, scientific planning, effective control and continuous monitoring. The Government policyon tourism has shown, at least theoretically, sensitivity to the environmental concerns. The Tourism Policy of 1982 and guidelines on ecotourism aim to achieve some of the following objectives, that:

(a) the level of development is compatible with the general capacity of the physical environment and resources;

(b) sufficient facilities and services are provided to serve the tourists and the local population;

(c) the hotel rooms are distributed in such a manner that the natural characteristics and qualities of the area are enhanced;

(d) the tourism-related constructions are designed carefully and sensitively to merge with the surroundings to enhance the natural beauty; and

(e) the architectural heritage sites and other areas of historic value are protected adequately.

In the initial years of the development of ecotourism, greater emphasis was laid on the development of the Himalayas and the deserts in the State of Rajasthan. The mighty Himalayas encircling India in the north not only provide immensely diverse tourism attractions but also influence the climate, rainfall and the flow of rivers in India. Ecotourism in the Himalayan region, therefore, is the basic corner stone of ecotourism policy in India. The Himalayan Tourism Advisory Board (HIMTAB) was set up by the Government of India in 1987 as a voluntary consultative mechanism for mutual cooperation between the States in Himalayan region to promote integrated tourism. The Board meets at different places in the Himalayan States and formulates policies and programmes for the development of tourism in the region. The issues considered by the Board in various meetings so far include development of alternate resorts to reduce overcrowding in the established tourist spots, use of alternate sources of energy, registration of porters and guides and their training and motivation, coordination of mountain rescue operations, preservation of ecosystem, establishment of effective communication, efficient garbage disposal systems, safety and security of tourists, etc. It is recognised that as a first step in the development of tourism, haphazard growth has to be checked and a future strategy has to be properly planned. India being a federal polity composed of many States and Union Territories, the idea of a National Master Plan is not a feasible one. At the national level, therefore, an attempt is made to collate the Master Plans of the States and to coordinate the activities of different States in tune with the national policy of sustainable development. In addition, to ensure that environmental and ecological needs are carefully nurtured and that in the name of tourism development, the fragile ecosystem is not exploited in too many small schemes, a strategy of 'Special Tourism Area' has been devised by the Government of India. Under this scheme, the State Governments are required to identify and notify suitable areas as 'Special Tourism Area' so that comprehensive development plans for such areas can be taken up. The identification of such areas is done on the basis of its tourism potential and the ability to attract private investment for its development on a commercial basis. The Government's involvement in such Special Tourism Areas should be only to the extent of providing the basic infrastructural development. The States of Kerala, Orissa and Maharashtra have developed such Special Tourism Areas. Currently, the Government of India is encouraging various forms of tourism which have direct impact on preservation of heritage and culture; developing Heritage Railway Tourism in Rajasthan, Gujarat and Darjeeling; creation of amusement parks, science cities, and providing an impetus to the promotion of industrial tourism, are but a few steps in this direction. Fairs like "Suraj Kund Mela" based on the concept of craft and ethnicity have been big draws with the tourists. The Government of India's assistance for promoting local initiative through regional fairs and festivals not only provides for growth of tourism through economic impetus for the local community, but also facilitates inter-regional interaction within the country.

Regulations and Sustainability

While the major emphasis in the development of sustainable tourism is on public participation and involvement, it is essential that the Government plays the role of coordinating and controlling the activities to arrive at the objectives defined. Alive to this requirement, a number of regulations have already been put into place by the Government of India. Many of these legislations are designed to protect ecologically fragile and sensitive ecosystems. Some of the important ones among them are:

(i) Forest (Conservation) Act, 1980 which controls the use of forests for non-forestry uses.

(ii) Wildlife (Protection) Act, 1972 which designates the National Parks and Wildlife Sanctuaries and stipulates a comprehensive framework for wildlife protection and conservation.

(iii) Environment Protection Act, 1986 stipulates

several measures for protecting and improving the quality of the environment and preventing, controlling and abating environmental pollution. Coastal Regulation Zones (CRZ) were gazetted by a notification under the Act in 1991 and a wide range of activities have been prohibited in the sea coast within 500 metres of High Tide Line (HTL).

Guidelines for Ecotourism

In addition to the above regulations, recently the Government of India have worked out certain broad guidelines for ecotourism which stipulate that the developmental process itself should meet the following cardinal principles—

(i) It should involve the local community and lead to the overall economic development of the area.

(ii) It should identify areas where conflicts may arise because the resource used for promotion of tourism may be the same from which local community get their livelihood. Ecotourism policy attempts to minimize such conflicts by finding ways to balance needs for development with necessity of preservation.

(iii) The type and scale of tourism development should be compatible with the environment and socio-cultural characteristics of the local community.

(iv) Ecotourism policy should be planned as a part of the overall area development strategy and should be guided by an integrated land use plan. It should not be seen as something alien to environment.

The guidelines for ecotourism development planning also cover many other important issues. Some of the salient features can be briefly mentioned as:

(a) Decisions for the development of tourism in ecologically fragile areas have to be based on a thorough understanding of local resources, social and economic factors and other characteristics. The objectives of tourism development in any specific area as well as the intended beneficiaries, have to be decided on the basis of these factors and on the strength of discussions and negotiations with those most directly concerned.

(b) The development of physical infrastructure for tourism should be preceded by the preparation of an inventory of the available resources and a careful zoning/management plan to ensure proper use and preservation of valuable natural sites.

(c) Wherever for tourism development, destruction or serious alteration of areas of high primary productivity like wetland, seagrass beds, coral reefs, rain forests becomes necessary, careful social and economic cost-benefit analysis should precede any such planning. Further, planning and promotion of tourism should be undertaken as a component part of an integrated, comprehensive resource management plan based on sound ecological principles.

(d) The 'Tourism Management Plan' should also establish standards for resort development, covering among others, the style and locations of structures, treatment of sewage and control of litter, preservation of open spaces and public use of fragile areas. It should further lay down procedures to ensure that sewage is not directed to the beach and that the groundwater and solid waste like litter, garbage, trash, etc., are systematically collected and disposed suitably. The planning and regulatory process should carefully go into various details that have bearing on the ecology and should specify methods for construction materials to be used for such construction, encourage use of eco-friendly local materials, minimise noise pollution, etc.

(e) Physical planning and design should integrate community services, transportation and tourism. There are numerous instances of community life style being adversely affected and hardship caused to them because of pressure on limited civic amenities when influx of tourists takes place without proper planning for civic services, transportation, etc.

Ecology and Tourism: A Vision of the Future

It would be pertinent to ponder over what the global community and the Government of India can do to ensure that the rich inheritance is enhanced and enriched and passed on to the future generation instead of being debased and eroded in mindless commercial exploitation. Indian tourism today is based primarily on either the gift of nature or what history has bestowed over thousands of years. In a developing country like India, with such tremendous pressure of population, there is eagerness and struggle for economic betterment as quickly as possible. Tourism provides many avenues for quick earnings. For a national policy, there cannot be any two opinions about preserving the surroundings for the benefit of the present and the future generations. But for many engaged in daily struggle for survival, considerations of today's earnings take precedence over thoughts for tomorrows's heritage. They would find much philosophical truth in the famous statement of Lord Keynes that "in the long run we are all dead". One of the greatest challenges for tourism planning today, therefore, is to achieve that amount of public motivation where exploitation of the environment and ecosystem do not exceed the accepted optimal level of carrying capacity. There is, therefore, an urgency in dovetailing the short-term gains from tourism exploitation of the ecosystem with the long-term compulsions of maintaining the ecosystem. Conscious and serious efforts, therefore, will have to be made to find a balance between these two conflicting trends and to take concrete steps to preserve the heritage which is not renewable. There is already consciousness all around the globe on these issues. This con: ciousness perhaps needs to be developed into a common durable vision and to evolve some ideology to pursue. It is perhaps necessary to create a movement to spread the ideologies and to take them beyond the realm of usual declarations of intent. Perhaps the 600 million tourists that go round the globe annually today — and that number is swelling — be made the ambassadors of such a global movement for creating awareness for a sustainable tourism development. Most developing countries face the dilemma that the absolute cost of protecting the socio-cultural and ecological environment is too high and at the same time the cost of not developing such heritage for economic use also is too high to ignore. Even to translate the nation's honest intentions regarding eco-friendly tourism into action, trained manpower, pool of experts and professionals are needed whose services can be used to blend the economic needs with sustainable development. Many nations do not have the resources to acquire such expertise. Naturally serious sustainable development movements would also need resources and most nations who need such movements do not have such resources. Lord Keynes had the vision to mastermind the creation, out of the despair of the war ravaged world of two institutions—the World Bank and the International Monetary Fund (IMF)—which continue to provide hope and ideas to the world. Before our inheritance on which tourism revolves run the risk of irreparable damage, it is time to think of such an international organisation which can not only provide the ideology but also would be instrumental in providing resources to shape that ideology into a meaningful action plan. All across the globe, there are millions of people who still share such ideas and would be willing to join hands in making such a vision a reality. India can make a beginning in this regard.

Sustainable Heritage Tourism

The word 'heritage' means an inheritance or legaly; things of value which have been passed from one generation to the next. In tourism the term 'heritage' has come to means not only landscape, natural history, buildings, artefacts, cultural traditions and the like which are either literally or metaphorically passed on from one generation to the other, but those among these things which can be portrayed as tourism products like cultural heritage, particularly architecture, historic sites and artistic monuments.. Fortunate, India, being the cradle of many religions and abode of an rulers has a number of monuments and historic sites. The art and architecture of Hindu, Buddhist, Jain and Islamic monuments have been acclaimed world widely. People from all walks of life come to India to see the rich variety of architecture since time immemorial. The Archaeological Survey of India (ASI), is the only national agency at the centre which takes care of monuments as far as conservation of depleted monuments and eroded sculptures are concerned. A few years back India National Trust for Art and Culture Heritage (INTACH) was formed as a Non Government Organisation and it has initiated to take up the work of conservation of neglected historic buildings. But the impacts of increased number of visitors, surrounding industries, local persons and other physical and cultural menace on heritage buildings have not checked effectively. It could lead to serious disaster and a loss of valuable cultural tourism products.

Role of UNESCO and Heritage Preservation in India

India is a grand repository of ancient cultural and natural treasures of exceptional value. It was indeed a memorable day in 1972 in the sphere of International Co-operation when the General Conference of UNESCO adopted a resolution with overwhelming enthusiasm creating thereby a Convention concerning the protection of this World Cultural and Natural Heritage. The main objective of this forum is to :

- define the World Heritage in both cultural and natural aspects.
- enlist Sites and Monuments from the Member countries which are of exceptional interest and universal value, the protection of which is the concern of all mankind.
- promote co-operation among all Nations and people to contribute for the protection of these universal treasures intact for future generations.

The list of recorded sites on the World Heritage now stands at 288 which include both cultural and natural wonders, an endowment that is shared by all mankind and the protection of which is the concern of the entire mankind. As on May 1987, 95 countries have joined this forum. India is an active member State on the World Heritage from 1977 and has been working in close co-operation with other International agencies like ICOMOS (International Council of Monuments and Sites), IUCN (International Union for the Conservation of Nature and Natural Resources) and ICCROM (International Centre for the study of the Preservation and Restoration of Cultural Property). It is an elected member on the World Heritage Committee since 1985 and is contributing regularly for the promotion of World Heritage. It has inscribed already 13-Cultural Sites and 4-Natural ones. The Cultural Sites are Ajanta Caves (153), Ellora Caves (154), Agra Fort (155), The Taj Mahal, Agra (156), The Sun Temple, Konark (185) Mahabalipuram Group of Monuments (240), Hampi Monuments (241), Fatehpur Sikri, Mughal City (242), Group of Monuments at Pattadakal (260), Elephanta Caves (265), and Brihadisvara Temple, Thanjavur (266). The Natural Sites are Kcoladeo National Park (212), Manas Wildlife Sanctuary (213), Kaziranga National Park (214), and Sunderbans National Park, (215). The ICOMOS, a wing of UNESCO, has declared April 18 of every year as a World Heritage Day. The Department of Culture and Archaeological Survey of India, apart from observing this World Heritage Day and augmenting various practical measures in respect of conservation of the World Heritage Monuments, have decided to observe the World Heritage Week from 19th November every year coinciding with the birthday of Smt. Indira Gandhi, the late Prime Minister of India, whose love and concern for the cultural and Natural Heritage was too well known. It is specially aimed to involve the youth of the country through NSS/NCC units in such works as protection, preservation and propagation of the great heritage for which our country is justly world famous. The international workshop Managing Tourism in Natural World Heritage Sites organized by UNEP and UNESCO in Dakar, Senegal in November, 1993 developed the following Ten Commandments for protecting World Heritage sites of the country.

- Tourism development should consider and respect the ecological and socio-cultural values of the site and should be consistent with the World Heritage concept.
- A management plan, considering the regional context and tourism component, should be established and regularly updated.
- Environmental assessments, including cumulative impacts, should be carried out on recreational and commercial facilities and activities before approvals are granted.
- Monitoring programmes based on appropriate and updated indicators should take place and their outcome should be taken into account in the planning and decision-making process.
- Local populations, in and around the site, should be involved in order that they take pride in their heritage and benefit from tourism.
- Co-operation with the different stockholders involved in tourism development should be sought to ensure co-ordination for the promotion of the site.
- All site staff should be aware of World Heritage values and well trained in visitor management.
- Relevant information and educational programmes should be put in place to ensure

that visitors and local people understand and respect the site.

- A substantial portion of the income generated through entrance fees should be directly allocated to the site for its improvement and management.
- Each site should participate in the promotion of the World Heritage concept through all appropriate means.

This has been undenying fact that the impact of tourism on ecology and environment as also on social milieu, cannot be ignored as money can buy infrastructure but cannot always buy style and natural charm. This definitely calls for working out a happy compromise between two extremes, whether or not to promote tourism at the cost of environmental—natural and human-degradation or to preserve environment for no tourism through a forceful, well-conceived, defensible and amenable-to-implementation policy. Therefore it is the 'Sustainable Tourism Development' (STD) which should, and needs to be more adequately stressed and promoted, as against the present tendency to pamper conventional international tourism, in the interest of the tourism industry as such and that of the economy as whole.

It is quite difficult to perceive the definition of STD as it is elusive being a recent introduction. It involves working for the long-term viability and quality of both natural and human resources. It is certainly not anti-growth, but admits limits to growth. Sustainable Tourism Development implies that Exploitation of Resources, Direction to Investment, and Orientation of Technology should be in consonance with the needs of the present and future. It is significant to note that Tourism continues to grow at a dramatic rate at the global level and the increasing pressure of tourist traffic naturally aggravates the degradation of the environment and social milieu.

A happy compromise has to be worked out in-between the two extremes: whether to promote tourism at the cost of environmental degradation or to preserve environment for "no tourism" through a forceful, well-conceived, defensible and amenable-to-implementation policy. To solve these problems, appropriate development strategy for achieving environmentally sustainable tourism is the right choice. Besides, there may be problem of socio-cultural pollution, in case tourism is not set on sustainable tourism track. Otherwise, long-term environmental (natural and human) consequences shall be easily passed off for a marriage of convenience.

The drive for the increase in tourism is based primarily on economic benefits, not on whether such levels of tourism are sustainable. The environmental and social impacts of the unprecedented tourism boom call for an eventual shift to a comprehensive regional strategy that sets limits to growth in order to sustain socially and environmentally compatible tourism. Notably, it is the 'Sustainable Tourism Development' which needs to be more adequately stressed and promoted, as against the present tendency to pamper international tourism, in the interest of the tourism industry as such and that of the economy as whole. Because it is the complexity of tourism in its interactions with other sectors of the economy and with natural and cultural environment that highlights the complexities and intricacies of sustainable tourism. The need at present is for quality control as tourism must be recognised as a resource valuable, long-term and renewable.

Infact, sustainable tourism is a positive approach intended to reduce the tensions and friction created by the complex interactions between the tourism industry, the visitors, the environment and the communities which are host to holiday makers. It involves working for the long-term viability and quality of both natural and human resources. It is certainly not anti-growth, but acknowledges that there are limits to growth. Thereupon, to ensure that tourism does not lead to a loss of environmental and cultural identity, but is rather a source of mutual enrichment, it must be well pondered over by states and the people on a universal scale. Sustainable Tourism Development contributes to human well-being while maintaining harmony with environment as it implies preservation and conservation of tourist resources; preservation of national heritage and conservation of natural environment.

Inskeep (1991) opines that 'tourism researchers and planners are increasingly recognising that successful tourism development must sustain the community's socio-cultural, natural and built environments as well as contribute to economic well-being. The basic economics of tourism must be planned according to the sustainability and present carrying capacity of touristic areas for future need.

While Hawkes and Williams (1993) state that 'the concept of sustainable tourism embodies a challenge to develop the world's tourism capacity and the quality of its products without adversely affecting the environment that maintains and nurtures them'. In the Brundtland Report on Our Common Future, sustainability is defined as 'the idea that the needs of today's visitor should not be met at the expense of future generations'. Urban planners feel that sustainable tourism makes a strong plea for blending tourism in urban planning system so as to minimise the adverse effects of over-urbanisation. In view of socio-cultural impacts and the level of resentment created thereby, community's participation in formulating, executing and monitoring the development programmes is surely the best bet. Creating awareness and a sense of belonging amongst the various agents and actors in the industry and the visitors can ensure tourism culture, one of the basics of tourism development. An overall view of successful and sustainable tourism development calls for a synergistic relationship of community's involvement, planning and technical assistance.

Shift in STD Paradigms

The rather rapid and substantial changes in the nature of tourism and broad recognition of its inter-relationship with natural environment necessitate new paradigms to manage tourism development. The unprecedented development of tourism especially during the last quarter of the 20th century has obviously evoked concerns about social, cultural and environmental impacts of tourism at the global level in general, and at the national level, in particular. Could there be a way of alliance between the conflicting 'target groups' and policy enforcement organisations where communality and consensus of interests may lead to some kind of righteous tourism package that fits in the philosophy of Sustainable Tourism Development? Gunn (1988) suggests four perspectives in this context, viz., those of the tourists, the developers, the providers of services, and the local resident community. In this context, alternative forms of tourism have been experimented with fair measure of success in some of the countries, under different titles, such as Green Tourism, Soft Tourism, Responsible Tourism, Appropriate Tourism, Rural Tourism.

Heritage Tourism, Cultural Tourism, Defensive Tourism, Community based Tourism, Craft Tourism, etc., but the spirit behind them all is most humanising, and development of tourism sums up its basis (Shades of Green, 1990).

Carrying Capacity

No doubt, each destination has a certain optimum carrying capacity which would have to be properly estimated and provided for. One of the paradigms suggested for ascertaining sustainable tourism development is through fixing the carrying capacity of the area and limiting the number of visitors per day, besides limiting the length of stay in hotel, especially in core areas. While the carrying capacity of the physical and social environment has really become a perennial issue as environment is the ecological capital of tourism. The degradation of environment that can occur through poorly planned ad hoc development must be addressed urgently. Moreover, concerns are frequently expressed about the social and cultural impacts of tourism and recreation development, thus carrying capacity must also include a social component as well. Impacts on the social carrying capacity of the local community through inadequate information, lack of affordable housing, increased taxes and cost of living, and resentment towards tourism, etc., could occur in case the rate of change was faster than the community could accommodate. These obviously highlight the importance of guide training programmes, multilingual regional guide books, and awareness of the types of historic, cultural and landscape resources that appeal to the foreign guests. Carrying capacity paradigm fails to be an effective and useful approach as a planning tool as it has significant conceptual and practical weaknesses. Mass tourism may not always be undesirable or inappropriate and, by the same standard, small scale tourism may not, ipso facto, be sustainable. Thereby, Limits of Acceptable Change Process focussing on management of impact instead of visitor numbers could be the alternative.

The Limits of Acceptable Change Planning System

Infact, the Limits of Acceptable Change (LAC) is a planning framework meant for identifying the intrinsic complexity of development issues without being as reductionistic as the carrying capacity paradigm. It deals with the identification of desired conditions and means to attain them. The system is built upon several premises: First, any human use of a natural environment results in some change in that environment and the others affected by it.

Therefore, planning and management are expected to focus on identifying how much human-induced change—in both natural and social conditions—is acceptable. Second, diversity in natural and social conditions is both inevitable and desirable. Therefore, planning needs to consider that conditions acceptable in one case may not be desirable in others as each location has a unique biophysical character and a socio-political setup.

It further implies that different outcomes may be expected in different situations even from the same process. Management and Planning focus on achieving certain desired economic-societal and environmental conditions through a well-defined planning process. These outputs tend to explain what it is that is to be sustained. Each sphere has its won economic, societal and environmental limits for which the tourism growth continuum may not be tenable, be it the traditional mass tourism or even apparently more salutary alternate forms of tourism. Hence a well-informed and judicious tourism policy with an appropriate and efficient development planning systems can be of help to direct tourism development in the desired direction, though within the given limits. A thoughtful deliberation of the economic, social and environmental limits/conditions acceptable to the community and the manner in which tourism development will be useful to the community are both significant while considering any tourism development plan/ strategy and/or its implementation in efficient manner.

Alternative Tourism

Basically, alternative tourism aims at seeking a transition from impersonal, traditional mass tourism to establishing cordial rapport between visitors and the local hosts. It is primarily related to the scale of development in terms of product indigenisation, healthy interaction amongst people, local control and an attempt to bring back the lost art of travel. In this context, the criteria for considering suitability of a region may be alterable but Williams (1990) has marked certain factors to be taken note of while fixing the criteria which includes the following.

- Efficiency and effectiveness of desired product output;
- Influences on regional economic growth;
- Influence on local resident's quality of life;
- Use of locally available factors of production; and
- Harmony with the local, social and cultural structures.

Again, in the context of the use of locally available factors, it is worth mentioning that tourism, being a highly competitive business, forces and developers to go for hard technologies which, besides furnishing quality infrastructure, make the rate of development brisk and meet the volume of traffic. These are, generally, not only costly but are also unfriendly to environment in gross way.

Multi Destination Development

It is significant to note that the competive world of tourism trade warrants a constant development of new and exclusive attractions along with upgradation of the existing ones. The Multi Destination or Decentralized Destination Development or Destination Region—a number of satellite destinations with a prime destination-concept now gaining currency in both developed and developing countries, not only ensures maximum satisfaction to the tourist by influencing the consumer's choice for multi destination travel patterns. Apart from economic gains, it is also quite likely to offer a helping hand to the host country in the terms of working for the long-term viability and quality of both human and natural resources through a dispersal of the negative imapcts of mass tourism over a number of destinations of the region and, thus, leading to 'Sustainable Tourism', the ultimate in the context.

Heritage Tourism

As a recent development, 'Heritage tourism' had developed as an international phenomenon, based on the historical and cultural resources of tourism destinations. It seems to fall into two categories—tourism to places of genuinely high esteem for their historical and environmental importance and tourism to nostalgia where heritage tourism is more important as a marketing approach and a promotional theme than genuinely significant. In a greater acceptance of change and awareness of the importance of history and environmental future, heritage tourism has to play an important role in supporting communities in their quest for sustainable development. An active international organisation, UNESCO, has choose to conserve and preserve ten extra-ordinary resources for posterity.

Cultural Tourism

Practically, cultural tourism development is community-based, participatory and designed to improve the economic and social well-beging of local residents in addition to the concerned institutional and physical environment. It also pin-points the need for careful planning to protect the integrity of sites and minimise harmful impacts. Moreover, the host community needs to plan ahead to ensure that cultural tourism sustains and benefits local communities socio-culturally as well as economically and is not meant simply for minting money for governments or private entrepreneurs.

The cultural tourist wants to discover the country and its culture with comprehensive understanding and to achieve all this he expects knowledgeable explanation, interaction and feed-back.'

If, instead of going for commercialisation of culture, tourism endeavours to satisfy its obligations towards society and culture, it will be more than a step forward towards the desired end. Frohlich (1993) advocates a conceptual transition from 'Culture in Tourism consists in the modesty and patience of the host community towards the foreign guest' to one where 'Culture in Tourism is the modesty and open mindedness of the traveller towards the host community and its cultural situation'.

For this, an open dialogue between the two, i.e., society and tourism, can go a long way in ensuring the sought-after end in the right spirit.

Priorities in Planning

Of course, countries should determine their national priorities and tourism's role in a proper 'hierarchy' of priorities to devise its optimum tourism strategy. This strategy should define, amongst others, the balance to be sought between tourism development and environment; take into account the carrying capacity of the destinations; and the roles of State, Regional and Local Organisations. Within the overall national tourism strategy, priority attention should be given to selective and controlled development of tourist infrastructure, facilities, demand and overall tourist capacity in order to protect the environment and local resident population, so as to minimise, if not avoid, any negative impacts which unplanned tourism might produce. In tourism planning and area development, it is essential for states to strike a harmonious balance between economic and ecological considerations.

In this connection, it worth while to quote Mings (1978) who suggests that governments have three possible options related to tourism :

(i) The "no change" option: ignore the problems and prospects;

(ii) Withdraw public support for tourism and even attempt to curb private promotion of tourism; and

(iii) Pursue retionalisation of the industry to make it more beneficial.

Obviously, of the three, the last option seems to be the most reasonable in general. It involves an assessment of the problems and prospects and a plan of action to redress weaknesses and to direct the industry towards long-term goals. Wilkinson (1989) however, raises two pertinent issues about the above proposition. First, can the various problems related to tourism be put right satisfactorily ? The answer in the affirmative lies in the shift in the stance of the government from tourism development based on immediate gains, i.e., short-term prospect for earning foreign exchange and job creation to long-term economic, social and environmental viability, i.e., sustainable development. Second, in case the answer seems to be affirmative, will contributions (economic, social and environmental) of outliving tourism industry be adequate enough to justify public support ? Murphy (1985) contends that only when the needs of the local resident community are given priority over the goals of tourism industry, can a positive response be expected. This is, indeed, nothing but the community approach of tourism intended to put forth a "Community Tourism Product" — a synthetic blend of the destination's resources and facilities which the community is prepared to offer to the tourism market. This is, in fact, drawing near to Farrell's (1986) notion of "Cooperative Tourism" — a consortium of active players — local people, industry managers, government and visitors — sharing responsibilities and rewards.

Preservation of Heritage & Culture

The fairs and festivals reflect the vast cultural heritage of India and have, for that reason been a tremendous draw with the tourists over the years. In the draft of National Action Plan for Tourism, May 1992, it has been recommended that the government should make efforts to organise cultural evenings, son-et-lumieres, Craft bazars, food plazas and fairs and festivals at important tourist destinations all round the year by having a tie-up with zonal cultural centres. 'Teej' celebration by Rajasthan Tourism Development Corporation is a stance in this direction. However, in view of the objective of culture reservation night stay has been disallowed, e.g. in the close neighbourhood of Dilwara temple in Rajasthan. In other words, provisioning of tourist accommodation and other related entertainment facilities is not required. This will certainly help maintain the religious sanctity and cultural identity of the tourist destination. On the other hand, there are a large number of Palaces and *Havelies* lying in a state of disrepair and neglect that can very conveniently be converted into 'Heritage Hotels'. This will certainly be a foot forward in the preservation of national heritage. Till date, some headway has already been made in this regard, but very much more can be, and need to be done.

Involving Community

Community participation and grass-root planning are, indeed, the pre-requisites for community-based tourism development. The earlier occurrence of failure of sustainable tourism development in Goa can be attributed to the denial of rights to the indigenous hosts. Returning of the over-wrought coast lands for restoration and preservation to the local community called 'folk ecologists', continuous and regular community involvement in planning, monitoring and evaluation provesses with an objective of creating awareness and a sense of belonging, and launching of 'learn to travel campaigns' are some of the possible measures that can provide the most potent solutions. The Goan community's involvement in Carnivals, fairs and festivals are a testimony that the local people are conversant not only with the benefits of the environment but also the need to preserve it.

Sustainable Tourism and Carrying Capacity

The process of Sustainable Tourism has already started

in the form of Island tourism in Andamans and Lakshadweep islands. It has been decided that a few islands on selective basis will be opened out for tourism purposes keeping in view their carrying capacity and the constraint to preserve their environment. The emphasis will be on high-value low-volume tourist traffic to the selected islands and the facilities to be provided would blend with the natural beauty of the islands.

Environmental Preservation

Since ancient times, Indian culture has taught men to love and respect nature, seeing themselves as part of it. Wildlife conservation, too, had its origin in India in the remote past as killing animals and felling of trees were not only illegal but were considered anti-social and irreligious. Uttar Pradesh, India's most populous state, despite pressing demographic and economic needs, took a lead in the modern conservation movement. The establishment of India's first National Park (Hailey National Park [now Corbett National Park (CNP) and Corbett Tiger Reserve (CTR) in 1935 has indeed been a landmark. Nanda Devi National Park (NDNP) with an area of 2000 sq.kms, the highest national park of the country and the second highest in the world after Sagarmath National Park of Nepal, was set up on November 6, 1982. Moreover, in the same region, Valley of Flowers, being a fabulous unique natural rock-garden with over 250 identified genera of flowering plants is the youngest high-altitude reserve of the country and is a favourite of the tourists. To protect and conserve this heritage, the Valley and its environment with an area of 87.5 sq.kms was declared a national park on November 6, 1982. However, Considering the environmental damage done to the Corbett National Park and Tiger Reserve by the ever-increasing number of visitors, the entry is being now regulated through advance booking available at Ramnagar (Nainital) only. Moreover, to check the garbage dumping problem, a bag is supplied to each visitor at the entry point and its carrying has been made mandatory.

Awareness Creation

Realising the cruciality of the need for creation of adequate awareness of the multi-dimensional impacts of tourism and providing relevant information to the local community, at the grass-root level, the government of India seems to have given it a serious thought. The outcome is in the form of introduction of tourism as a core faculty at the 10+2 level, in addition to various study programmes on pollution in the curriculum of school education from primary level onwards and audiovisual programmes on the national network.

Tourism is capable of destroying itself if not properly planned. The well-known aphorism that "tourism destroy tourism" has duly to be taken care of through efficient planning. Proper planning of the strategy for tourism development as also for any other sector, tourist or general, would, therefore, seem to be of paramount importance. A well thought-out and formulated plan/strategy would go a long way towards ensuring a successful take-off and sustenance of the tourism project. Further, while the plan/strategy would, as a matter of course, work out and incorporate the various cost-benefit and economic effects of the tourist development, it must also anticipate, and accommodate, the various likely effects of the development the environs, viz., its impact on the social, cultural and environmental milieu. Tourism development is, in this regard, like a double-edged sword: it can be of great benefit but it can also be a source of great stress. This brings out the cruciality of the need for community involvement, as all travel is essentially linked with communities, in tourism development planning and, especially, sustainable development planning.

3

BASICS OF SUSTAINABLE TOURISM PLANNING

> "Whatever I take from the Earth may have quick growth again. Purify, may we not injure the vitals of Thy heart."
>
> —*Atharvaveda*

As a management technique, there are certain basic factors which are to be taken into consideration in the planning process. First of all, there must bean objective and that objective must be clearly understood and accepted by all those who are to be involved. Secondly, there must be a programme leading to the objective. Lastly there must be a measurement of progress towards the objective set. The key factors, therefore, for a successful planning are the objectives, programme and the measurement of the objective.

Essentially, planning attempts to allocate scarce resources between different competing uses with a view to maximising output, income and employment and to ensure the balanced growth of different sectors. Such planning may be at an individual level or at a firm level or an industry level, or for the economy as a whole. There are broadly two economic systems prevailing in the economy: Planned economy and Market economy. Planned economy is one in which each production unit (or a firm) uses only the resources of men, material and equipment allocated to it by quota and disposes of its products to persons or firms indicated to it by simple order. On the other hand a market economy is controlled by the forces of market, like demand, supply, prices, transport, etc. Planning can be applied to any type of economic system, whether centrally structured or built up of many units of purely market economy character.

Planning for Tourism

Planned development in is of paramount importance in the field of tourism. Many countries in the world, especially the developing countries, have lately realised the importance of tourism and the benefits which it brings out. The use of microeconomic planning techniques for tourism sector is however relatively new. The planning methods for national economic development which have been largely utilised since the end of World War II did not always cover tourism development as a particular field. The increasing significance of tourism as a source of income, employment generation, regional development and as a major factor in the balance of payments for many countries has been attracting increasing attention on the part of many governments as well as others with an interest in economic development. Thus, tourism development became more and more a particular field of research in the economic planning undertaken by many countries. As far back as in the year 1962 the Secretary General of the United Nations had declared,' Impressive unanimity has been achieved regarding the potential value of development planning. The German social scientist, Sigmund von Radecki, wrote on the expanding growth of tourism:

> Travel today is the most popular form of happiness. Perhaps this has something to do with the fact that a

> large part of humanity these days is incarcerated in prisons of one sort or another. Or perhaps it might be more correct to say that travel is one of the focal points of happiness. For, if you ask the man in the street, what would you do if you won a big sweepstake? You generally receive one of the two replies: Either "Oh, I would travel see the world", or "I would build myself a house." These two replies, apparently contradictory, are unanimous in expressing two fundamental human longings for faraway places and home, sweet home. And in this, they bear the same relationship to each other as breathing in and out.

Further, as a recent development, Holiday travel has become the most conspicuous phenomenon of our time. Neither mass migration nor the world wars have succeeded in putting so many million people on the road as the desire for a holiday does year after year. People voluntarily leave their homes to enjoy their vacation in distant places. For more and more people in the industrial countries of the world, an annual holiday trip is an accepted way of life.

In Germany, holiday tours took the top spot in 'consumer hit parade', leaving behind savings and household purchases. In other words, holiday tours are the first item on the shopping list of a German household the erstwhile luxury has become a regular feature of life and a necessity. In Great Britain, seventy-five per cent of the British population took a holiday for four nights or more away from home in 1990. In the same year, fifty million short holidays of one to three nights away from home were taken. The, percentage in West Germany and Scandinavia is even higher. A holiday is the 'year's sugar allowance' in the bitterness of the industrial work-a-day world. Tourism has grown during the last fifty years in most areas of the world as an unplanned activity. The result has been haphazard and a sudden boost in tourism facilities like hotels, rail, air and road transport in places that become popular holiday resorts or to meet the demand to satisfy the profit instinct of the promoters. The patterns have been repeated in some Asian countries, especially in Japan, Thailand and Singapore. In Thailand, large hotels were built at a beach resort called Pattaya—about 150 kilometers, from Bangkok. Now, the occupancy of the hotels does not even average 50 per cent a year. Anyone, who has visited a few of these popular holiday resorts in the world, cannot but be aware of the depressing circumstances under which commercialisation has taken precedence over the care or protection of the landscape and environment. A large number of people are going to the same spot at the same time.

The serious situation caused by haphazard development has made people and the governments aware of the need for planning of tourism development based on scientific research of the requirements of the travel market and the capacity of the area to take in the tourists. The need for planning is paramount. We do not provide more seats to a plane or rooms in a hotel beyond its maximum capacity, taking into account the passenger's comforts. Why should a resort or an area be choked with people? Planning of tourism development, however, is of recent origin. It was specially taken note of during the last 65 years after public voices were heard against the unplanned invasion of tourism. In 1950, Gerhard Noble called mass tourism "one of the great western plagues hardly less evil in effects than the epidemics of the middle ages." In a conference held in Limuru, Kenya, the tourist inflow was referred to "as a dangerous invasion." These remarks, however, may be exaggerated apprehensions of the environmentalists, But no one disputes the fact that where modern industrial life makes inroads into ancient societies, traditional values begin to totter. Tourism is a form of social industrialisation with all its advantages and disadvantages. Its advantages have to be grasped and utilised with care so that the impact of the disadvantages is minimised. It is here that planning comes in.

Planning is of greater benefit to developing societies where tourism is a new phenomenon and has had little or no adverse effect so far. The World Bank warned as, early as 1972: In many areas of the world, tourism development, has produced, great disparities in the standards of amenities provided for the visitors and for the local population. This cannot be entirely avoided, but in the long run, the improvement of standards for the local population is probably a condition of successful tourism development. The development of a new resort by the provision of infrastructure costing perhaps millions of dollars has a great impact on land values in the area affected. Were these benefits to accrue largely to a few private landowners, the World Bank would have difficulty in financing such a project. The acquisition of land by government or a public agency prior to development... eases the problems of planning on an integrated basis, and of enforcing proper zoning and building regulations. It also helps to ensure that windfall gains do not accrue solely to private landowners and provides the opportunity for the public, agency to offer serviced sites to hotel developers at prices which can include, if necessary, an incentive element.

Significanitly, there is a very dose relationship between land prices and building densities, and by appropriate land pricing the development authority can help to ensure that acceptable physical planning and density standards are maintained.' The statement makes two significant points:

- Tourism planning should not be left totally to private enterprise in search of profit. Government must actively participate in it.
- Planning should be integrated to avoid as far as possible, disparities in the standards of amenities for the visitors and local population.

Uptil recent past, tourism planning was looked at from a simplistic point of view. Planning simply implied that new hotel construction should be encouraged, more airlines should start operation, promotional campaigns may be launched within the country and abroad and border crossing must be eased. Although it worked to some extent, it was at best an erratic method of planning tourism. That is how most developing countries started their own tourism planning, resulting in a number of mistakes.

Tourism has become a major industry in many countries of the world and has thus a pervasive effect on the economy of the nations as well as their social structure. Unplanned tourism can hamper, a nation in getting maximum benefits from its development. The development of the tourism sector is one of the several options before a government, making claims on its resources which, in most cases, are limited. It is, therefore, necessary for tourism planners to place their case before the government in justifiable terms listing anticipated contribution to the economic development of the country through tourism development.

Much canvassed two economic arguments in favour of developing tourism are:

- the contribution in terms of foreign exchange; and
- multiple employment potential of the tourism industry.

Tourism development has to be planned in relation to the total development of the country and the available resources.

Decision at the national level has to be taken by the government, preferably in consultation with various interests involved. A national policy is called for incorporating the directions in which tourism development should take place. The policy should also spell out national goals and objectives.

National objectives could be as under:

- Ensuring development at tourist centers and resorts consistent with the needs of each area.
- To develop infra- and super-structure to provide recreation facilities for visitors and the resident population.
- Preservation of cultural resources and the heritage.
- To maximise economic benefits in terms of improvements of standards of living of the people.
- Generation of new employment.
- Stimulation—of development at regional levels.
- Maximising visitors' satisfactions.

Basically, Tourism development is a complex phenomenon requiring in — depth study of resource and demand pattern in each country. The local visitors have their own preferences regarding what they want to do during their holidays. In

Great Britain, a 1990 study revealed that 60 per cent of domestic visitors go to the sea for their holiday which is accessible in a few hours from any part of the country. Fortunately, for Britain, most overseas visitors are not interested in sea holidays. For them, London is a tourist 'Mecca'. Some 10 million foreign visitors add to the congestion of London, annually, along with another 15 million domestic visitors. The French also prefer the sea. In the case of France, the sea is also the focus of attention of the foreign visitors adding to the congestion on its beaches. The Italians prefer the lakes, while the visitors opt for the history and culture of Rome and many other cities of Italy spreading millions of visitors thinly all over the country. India, as a large country, is in a position to distribute the tourists evenly though Delhi and Mumbai have pressure in peak winter months. The pattern of traffic has to be kept in mind while planning the development of tourism in a destination, especially at the supply side as it is not flexible. Hotels are not built in a day nor are the airports. It took Los Angeles several years to expand its airport to host the Olympics in 1984. For successful tourism planning, current and future supply has to be correlated to current and future demand.

Factors Responsible for Development

In fact, following are some of the factors which influence tourism development in a destination area·

- Size of the existing population.
- Diversity and vitality of already existing tourist activity.
- Whether the facilities were planned and planted in the area or grew spontaneously because of some man-made or national attraction.

- Availability of land and finance.
- Impact on the local community—benefits and social costs.
- Attitude of the local people towards the tourism projects.
- Magnitude and speed of development.
- Whether the area is extensive for future expansion or only limited expansion is possible.
- State of the local economy—options of alternate development.
- Availability of local manpower a dynamic population.

Resentment by local population against tourism projects, however beneficial to the community, can create problems, as it happened in Australia. Yeppon is a small town on the coast of central Queensland Australia's sunshine state described by its 6,000 inhabitants as 'Paradise'. It has beautiful views and miles of glorious beaches. A Japanese businessman saw the area and fell in love with it, deciding to develop it into a resort. The beach here is 10 times longer and wider than Waikiki in Honolulu. He bought 20,000 acres to develop it into an international resort, building a number of hotels, guest houses, wildlife parks and several other attractive features.

The scheme was approved by the Australian Government but the local residents did not like it. They could not tolerate the idea of thousands of tourists crowding their beaches all the year—round. The investor tried to woo the local population, offering them millions of dollars to build a retirement home and other facilities. In November 1981, a bomb exploded under a motel under construction destroying property. This is an example of the type of problems a developer can face—if local cooperation is not sought amicably.

Tourist Attractions

Planners must know what makes a tourist destination click. The following are some of the factors which would create tourist attraction:

Entertainment and Amusement

- Theatre, cinemas
- Local leisure, good food
- Night life
- Health resort, spa, springs
- Recreational/ Amusement parks,
- Zoo and ocean marinas
- Sporting activities, adventure sports

Scenic

- Wildlife, flora and fauna.
- Natural beauty.
- Attractive coastline/long beaches.
- Wildlife safari parks.
- Mountain location, rivers.

Climate

- mild temperature
- Duration of sunshine.

Cultural

- Ancient buildings, archaeological sites, history and culture.

- Religion
- Customs and traditions.

Way of Life

- Folk arts
- Handicrafts
- Traditional music
- Classical and folk dances
- Festivals/Fairs
- Art

Remarkably, any or many of these attractions excursions may lure visitors to a specific destination.

Research

Well-directed research is a precondition for planning in tourism. To utter dismay it is surprising that in the tourism field, an insignificant amount of money is spent on research compared to total turnover of tourism earnings. The spectacular tourism development in certain areas like Majorda in Spain or Hawaii in the USA was due to the fact that these were some of the first areas developed for a particular type of holiday. Today, they are no longer alone in the field. The sun, sea, sands and reasonable prices are available at other places too. Fast jets have made inexpensive travel possible to distant lands—like Sri Lanka, India, the Maldives, Thailand and Malaysia—where prices are much lower.

Therefore, for any new resort development, planning, both physical as well as economic considerations, are essential. A country which decides to develop tourism should take a hard look at places offering similar attraction, study their economics and call for specialists to prepare a tourism development plan. Competition must be identified. Technical assistance from foreign experts is useful as they can provide an objective assessment of the tourist resources of country.

The following include the aspects to be researched:

- Characteristics of the land available for development, and the price structure.
- Speed of construction to attract public investment.
- Possibility of direct and indirect taxes from tourism—related activities to justify public investment.
- Composition of the facilities to be provided—hotels, non-hotels and other services, industries like restaurants, stores and beach services.
- Total cost of infrastructure and superstructure in the area proposed to be developed. Infrastructure includes all forms of construction on and below the ground, that is, roads and parking areas, railway lines, airports, water supply, power houses and sewage disposal. Superstructure consists of hotels, motels, restaurants, entertainment, and shopping facilities etc.

In fact, Planning has to be done on two levels—national and local. At the national level the central government will be involved developing selected areas on the basis of research and study. The guiding principles in the selection of the areas are their marketability as tourist spots to international and domestic travelers, anticipated receipts from the tourism sector, and projections of future demand. The national plan shall also lay down the broad framework for development at local and regional levels. The detailed planning of the local needs has to be done at the local level though the central government may give financial assistance or subsidies to some of the activities. This arrangement is prevalent in countries where tourism is not highly developed and the state has to play a pivotal role. In India, although the government is involved in tourism planning, the private sector plays a significant role in developing tourist facilities.

Some of the facilities are planned, developed and managed solely by the state.

Now, most countries including China have opened their tourism sector for private participation. It may, however, be understood that a government cannot afford to do everything at once. They have to select priority areas for development where some infrastructure may exist and whose tourist attractions are relatively better known/The development of completely new areas, though a worthwhile proposition in time, has to take its turn depending upon the resources of the country and the political will to develop tourism on the part of the government.

In October 1977, the World Tourism Organisation published an inventory of tourism development plans of various countries. Out of the forty-three member—countries, which replied to the WTO questionnaire, thirty-seven had an integrated planning system at the national level. But in majority of the cases, the plans remained on paper and when these were acted upon, action was half-hearted or partial implementation. Some countries, like the United States and. Canada, have, strictly speaking, no national tourism plans. In the USA, a study for making federal policy and programme involvement in tourism more coherent and responsive to national interest was undertaken only in 1976. After six years of intensive efforts by the travel industry, President Ronald Reagan signed into law a National Tourism Policy Act on October 16,1981. Under this Act, the US Congress created the US Travel and Tourism Administration to 'optimise' the contribution of tourism and recreation industries to economic prosperity, full employment and international balance of payments to the US.

In Canada, each of the ten provinces and two territories are involved in tourism development planning. In USA, states are more actively involved in the promotion of tourism even more than the federal government. France has a full-fledged Ministry of Free Time which deals with tourism and leisure affairs.

So far, there has been little coordination and regulation in physical planning for tourism development. Resorts have developed in attractive settings while ancillary facilities like transportation were created belatedly to meet the demand. Industrial and commercial cities found themselves receiving more visitors. The new, substantial facilities created were shared by foreign visitors and the local people. Existing infrastructure designed for the requirements of a relatively static age came under the strain of anew and mobile society. The need for re-planning of the existing use of land and planning of new areas became paramount. This realisation, however, came only in the second half of the twentieth century.

In the similar vein, the transport revolution opened new regions of the world for touristic exploration. The tourism planners, therefore, had two different tasks: one of physical planning in new areas with potential but with little or no existing touristic activity, and the other of re-shaping the areas where tourism already existed. Secondly, re-planning of existing high density tourist areas. Where should the planners begin? The first thing is to analyse different types of national or other tourist resources of which each country has many—that could attract tourists. These may be of scenic beauty, history, a mystique, and so on. An inventory of all these resources of the country has to be made. Then, there are cities like London and Paris which have their own natural draw for visitors. As per one estimate, London, the biggest tourist attraction in the world, is visited by over 10 million tourists and Paris by about 20 million foreign visitors annually. After preparing the inventory, areas have to be selected for tourism development keeping in view the economic resources available. While taking up the areas for development in a city, it is necessary to define the minimum urban planning parameters which, if followed respected, may prevent the degradation of the environment through unregulated building activity. The Mediterranean seacoast is an example of such unregulated development leading to ugliness and confusion.

Significantly, basic parameters in planning a sea resort should indicate

(a) the space between buildings,

(b) the distance of the road from the beach; and the capacity of tourist accommodation on the beach or off the beach.

The guidelines should also give building specifications, length, suggested dimensions, and characteristics of the road network providing access to the sea. The creation and development of a green belt should be clearly marked. Non- regulated or unplanned structures should be allowed in the area proposed to be developed. Similarly, the tourism development plan of an area with historical monuments as a major attraction requires that the view of the monuments should not be concealed by any haphazard construction in the area surrounding the monument. For instance, no new construction should be allowed near the Red Fort, which may obstruct its view.

To conclude, the following must be considered in any area planning:

- Determination of broad parameters of urban planning and architectural specifications.
- Preparation of overall inventory of national tourist resources.
- Cost benefit studies of the proposed projects.
- Exploration of possibilities of investment in private and public sectors.

Investment and Income

'When a tourism project is taken up for implementation, the time relation between investment requirements—and revenue expectation has to be kept in mind.

Remarkably, the following 8-point project structure for tourism planning and development is recommended:

- Conceptual planning.
- Establishment of goals after a feasibility study.
- Market and resources analysis.
- Approval of the plan.
- Master planning.
- Staged implementation programme.
- Monitoring operations to ensure quality of services and operational success.
- The Evaluation and direction.

Systems must be established to provide continuing feedback on volume of tourism and levels of satisfaction provided. Such programmes are directed against decline of a destination.

Governments have to create a favourable climate for investment through regulations and fiscal measures. Since most private investors would expect a reasonable return on investment, special financial incentives are *necessary* to make tourism investment attractive. A tourism project needs to be assisted at two stages: first at the time of making investment, and subsequently at the operational stage. Participation in the development of a tourism plan by government may be more attractive to investors, if the government offers ' direct financial subsidy. Another form of help is special credit facilities for tourism projects as in countries like UK, France, Spain and India. A common form of credit is long-term loans for hotels at less than the market rates of interest. Since tourism financing is different from other industries, some countries have created special institutions to disburse such loans. France has Caisse Centrale de Credit Hotelier, Portugal has its Tourist Fund, Israel its Tourist Industry Development Corporation. In India, hotels are financed, on the recommendation of the Department of Tourism, by Industrial Finance Corporation of India (IFCI) at central level and State Financial Corporation at state level.

During late 1980's, an Indian Tourism Finance Corporation (TFCI) was created to finance tourism projects and it is doing a good job. Other organisations also continue to finance tourism projects. Tourism related industries could have a preferential rate of interest. Other alternate measures could be grant of interest rebate on tourism investment by making up the difference between the commercial rate and the rate proposed for the hotel industry. This is one of the several incentives given to hotels in recent years in India. Special facilities for the purchase of land at concessional rates for tourism superstructure can be a powerful incentive—especially in the backward regions of the country. Some governments recognise tourism as an export industry, as in India and offer same fiscal benefits and incentives as are available to other export industries. These include duty free import of equipment required for tourist services or reduction in customs duty or their waiver. The government can also make tourism investment attractive by giving tax relief at the operational stage to improve profitability. No tax for the first 2 to 5 years.

The Government can help tourism planning through manpower development by running hotel and tourism training schools/courses. Finally, the extent of government concessions to tourism is basically linked with the importance a state attaches to the tourism sector compared to other sectors of economy. The involvement of the government in tourism planning, development and promotion varies from country to country and region to region.

Government, Tourism and Environment

The control of planning of physical environment in tourism is imperative. The following points must be taken into consideration:

- What facilities should be erected and when?
- Alternative uses of land
- Pollution
- Serenity of atmosphere
- Integrity of landscape

- Cost of land and its ratio to building and development costs
- Traffic circulation
- Zoning and density
- Basic Services—water, electricity, gas, sewerage, etc.

Architectural style, building regulations, site—layout density, and preservation of the natural features of the land are part of the environmental control. Protecting lakes, hills, beaches, rivers and historical monuments from the onslaught of large masses of visitors are also the responsibility of the government. It is remarkable Vodic people in that age realised that the resources of the earth were not something which could be damaged at will. The following words of Krishna Chaitanya provide a warning: "If we do not realise that the beauty and variety of the earth are autonomous values in their own right, if we believe that we have life and health on earth and not with the earth, we will exploit it greedily and come to ruin speedily. If we treat the earth without reverence and ruin its beauty and order, the end will be the failure of the earth to produce any food for us. Demands for tourism are as diverse as the resources. It is not easy to match the supply with the demand, for tourism can create pressure on local facilities; can affect the landscape and the lifestyle of the people.

The problems of conservation were taken note of in the early stages of tourism development. America established the Yellowstone Park within an area of 3,350 square miles in 1872. The British founded a national trust for places of historic interest and national beauty in 1895. A separate Ministry of Town and Country Planning was created in

1943 in Great Britain. National Physical Planning began in the United Kingdom as early as in 1947 with the passing of Town and Planning Act. The National Park Access to the Countryside Act in 1949 established a National Park Commission with the objective of natural beauty and provision of opportunities for open-air recreation. The ten national parks created in England covered nine per cent of the land area. In 1971, a Department of Environment was set up in England.

In India, a Ministry of Environment and Forests was set up in 1985. The concern for preservation of ecological balance was not confined to the USA and the UK; it has its worldwide impact. In 1968, the Council of Europe launched the Air Pollution and Water Charter and Water Conservation Campaign. The African convention for conservation of nature took place in the same year. In the USA, the Council of Environmental Quality was established in 1970 and President Nixon promulgated, a 37—point programme of preservation of environmental quality. India is already facing problems relating to environment mainly due to pressure of population and only partly due to tourism. The case of Dal Lake in Srinagar (Kashmir) is burning evidence of this. No doubt, tourism can be a boon to any country, especially to a developing country like India or Nepal. But tourism planning has to ensure that India preserves be Himalayas in their original glory, and the wide variety of wildlife, which is a great asset for tourism. The government took a wise decision in banning the hunting of tiger, panther and other species which were in danger of becoming extinct due to wanton killing. The Tourist Development Council, an advisory body of the Government of India, in a resolution passed as early as 1972 at Goa, requested the Government of India to take steps to ensure that:

- Any new construction in the vicinity of monuments should meet aesthetic requirements.
- Any unnecessary interference from electric lines, power plants, petrol stations, and advertisement hoardings is avoided.
- Special care should be taken to prevent pollution of water and air, working of mines and quarries, dumping of domestic, commercial and industrial waste in the vicinity of monuments.
- Deforestation of the area around monuments is avoided.
- Financial assistance be given by the state governments, local bodies to improve and beautify roads and environment of monuments and other places of tourist attraction.
- To avoid haphazard peripheral growth, the location of facilities like canteens, book shops, curio shops, etc., in the vicinity of important monuments may be done only after clearance from the Archaeological Survey of India and the Department of Tourism.

As a follow-up on this resolution, the Department of Tourism selected ten archaeological complexes of tourist importance comprising thirty archaeological centers.

As part of the concern for tourism in relation to environment, TO conducted a survey of tour operators in United Kingdom about their views on environments. To a question whether tourists were concerned about the environmental quality of the destination they visit, 63 per cent of the tour-operators surveyed answered yes. In reply to another question whether they offered any products that might be classed 'environmental friendly' or 'Green', said yes. Seventy-nine per cent of the group said that they offered green products in Europe, 16 per cent in Asia Pacific, 13 per cent in Americas and 37 per cent in Africa. It seems that tour-operators were taking their business to alternate destinations from areas where environmental degradation was accentuating. Fifty-nine per cent said that they were moving their business from areas where environment was not safe.

Action for Planning

The first step towards sustainable planning and development is to protect the environment and initiate efforts for environment friendly tourism. Governments, in consultation with the Private Sector, can establish and enforce environmental standards for the travel and tourism. To facilitate and recognise this responsibility, the WTO has been developing key indicators for the tourism sector to improve decision-making with regard to sustainable tourism development (1996). Like a canary in a coal mine, indicators are used to warn of areas of concern so that action can be taken in time. Tourism currently lacks such a canary as the industry is multi-sectorial. It involves mass movement of people. The tourism product is affected by the actions and activities of many other sectors. A set of international environmental indicators similar to the well-accepted economic indicators has yet to be developed. The WTO has been sponsoring ground-breaking research in this field and has come up with a set of "environmental indicators" to measure the healthiness of tourism destinations. The idea is to devise simple measurements of environmental sensibility, stress on the environment, results of tourist use and the human and biological consequences of tourist use. They have been tested over the past year in pilot projects in the USA, Canada, Mexico, and the

Netherlands. The challenge has been to reduce the number of indicators, but at the same time include measures of all of the most important risks to the industry and the host region.

TABLE 1: **CORE INDICATORS OF SUSTAINABLE TOURISM**

Indicators	*Specific Measures*
1. Site Protection	1. Category of site protection according to IUCN index.
2. Stesss	2. Tourist number visiting site (per annum/peak month).
3. Use Intensity	3. Intensity of use-peak period (persons/hectares).
4. Social Impact	4. Ratio of tourists to locals (peak period).
5. Developing Control	5. Existence of environmental review procedure of formal controls over development of site and use densities.
6. Waste Management	6. Percentage of sewage from site receiving treatment (Additional indicators may include structural limits of other infrastructural capacity on site- e.g. water supply, garbage).
7. Planning process	7. Existence of organised regional plan for tourist destination region (including tourism component)
8. Critical Ecosystems	8. Number of rare/endangered species
9. Consumer Satisfaction	9. Level of satisfaction by visitors (questionnaire based)
10. Local Satisfaction	*10. Level of satisfaction by locals (questionnaire based).*

*International Union for the Conservation of Nature and Natural Resources.
Source: WTO (1995), Madrid

Determining Carrying Capacities. Carrying capacity analysis is believed the most reliable and effective method for Sustainable Tourism Development. The Importance of incorporating carrying capacity analysis into the tourism planning process has been emphasised, for example, by McCool (1978), Getz (1983), O'Reilly (1986), and Romeril

(1989) despite some difficulties in establishing precise means of measurement and standards. According to Inskeep (1991) carrying capacities need to be established generally for the planning area (usually based on analysis of the specific major attraction features, development sites, and sometimes tourist-transit points) and calculated more precisely for each development site at the community planning level. Inskeep (1991) emphasised the need to determine the carrying capacity of a destination so that tourism development:

- does not result in serious environmental problems such as congestion, air, water, noise or visual pollution, degradation of ecosystems, or overload of the infrastructure.
- does not result in a loss of cultural identity of the host society or social problems, such as crimes.
- does not create serious economic distortions, while still bringing economic benefits maintains tourist satisfaction levels so that the desired tourist market continue visiting the area.

According to WTO (1983) to determine the carrying capacity, the two aspects to be considered are:

The Indigenous Physical and Socioeconomic Environment: This refers to the capacity that can be achieved without resulting in damage to the physical (natural and man-made) environment and generating sociocultural and economic problems to the local community, and maintaining the proper balance between development and conservation.

The Tourism Image and Tourist Product: This refers to the capacity or number of visitors that are compatible with the image of the tourist product and the types of environmental and cultural experiences that the visitors are seeking. The criteria for determining optimum capacity levels include the following:

Physical

- Acceptable levels of visual impact and congestion;
- Point at which ecological systems are maintained before damage occurs;
- Conservation of wildlife and natural vegetation of both and land and marine environments; and
- Acceptable levels of air, water, and noise pollution.

Economic

- Extent of tourism that provides optimum overall economic benefits; and
- Level of tourism employment suited to the local community.

Infrastructure

- Adequate availability of transportation facilities and services;
- Adequate availability of utility services of water supply, electric power, sewage and solid waste disposal and telecommunications; and
- Adequate availability of other community facilities and services such as those related to health and public safety.

Socioculture

- Extent of tourism development that can be absorbed without detriment to the socioculture life styles and activities of the community; and

- Level of tourism that will help maintain cultural monuments, arts, crafts, belief system, customs, and traditions without detrimental effects.

Again, the criteria that can be applied in determining carrying capacities relative to tourism image or visitor satisfaction levels include the following:

Physical

- Overall cleanliness and lack of pollution of the destination environment;
- Lack of undue congestion of the destination environment, including of tourist attraction features;
- Attractiveness of the landscape or townscape, including quality and character of architectural design; and
- Maintenance of the ecological systems and flora and fauna of natural attraction features.

Economic

- Cost of the holiday and 'value for money'.

Sociocultural

- Intrinsic interest of the indigenous community and culture;
- Quality of local arts, handicrafts, cuisine, and cultural performances; and
- Friendliness of residents.

Infrastructure

- Acceptable standards of transportation facilities and services;

- Acceptable standards of utility services; and
- Acceptable standards of other facilities and services.

It is really problemation, how to determine the capacity standards for an individual tourist centre. For example, in the Mediterranean region, there is high beach usage whereas in tropical beach resorts like of Goa tourists spend much of their time around swimming pools in shaded areas rather than on the beach itself. Notably, Some standards for rural and recreation activities are cited by the WTO (1983) as follows, expressed in visitors per day per hectare except where noted:

- Forest park: up to 15.
- Suburban nature park: 15-70.
- High-density picnicking: 300-600.
- Low-density picnicking: 60-200.
- Sports/team games: 100-200.
- Golf: 10-15.

For water-based activities:

- Fishing/sailing: 5-30;
- Speed boating: 5-10; and
- Water skying: 5-15.

For nature trails in persons per day per kilometer:

- Hiking: 40; and
- Horse riding: 25-80.

Goa is the only region in India where WTO (1989) has conducted regional tourism carrying capacity study along with assessment of the social and environmental impacts of tourism and preparation of guidelines for control of planning and further development of this sector in the region. In formulating carrying capacity study, the beaches and their adjacent lands along with labour supply capabilities, infrastructure capacities, and social impacts evaluation were the primary consideration. It was estimated that an average density of 40 square metres of beach area per tourist bed would be an appropriate standard in assessing beach carrying capacity.

Assuming an average width of sandy beach of 40 metres, application of that standard means that not more than one bed running metre of beach should be developed. Additionally, it was decided that not more than 70 per cent of the beach or 46 out of 75 kms should be developed, in order to:

- Protect the general landscape character of the area.
- Protect the coastal villages and surrounding areas.
- Avoid ribbon or continuous development along with the coastline.
- Cater also for recreational.

Application of the standard of one metre of beach frontage per tourist bed to 46 Km results in an overall regional maximum development level of 46,000 tourist beds. As 30 per cent of beds of lower rate levels are expected to be constructed in places directly facing the beach and sea, not more than 35 Km of beach frontage are expected to be actually utilized for development. Based on assumptions made of future accommodation occupancy rates (75 per cent for domestic tourists and 50 per cent for foreign tourists) and average length of stay (4 to 5 days for domestic tourists and 15 days for foreigners) and a ratio of 80 per cent domestic and 20 per cent foreign tourists (aimed at increasing the proportion of foreign tourists through marketing and product development strategies), the 46,000 beds allowed would imply a level of approximately 4.1 million tourist arrivals annually, almost five times the 1988 level of tourists visiting the region (Inskeep, 1991).

Based on assumptions of direct employee requirements of 1.0 employees per bed (about 2.0 employees per room) in the upper classes of hotels and 0.4 employees per bed in other classes of accommodation based on the types of tourists attracted, the direct tourism sector employee requirement was calculated to be 60,000 persons, and the indirect emloyee requirement was calculated to be 30,000 (only twice the present number because of assumed greater productivity of workers in this sector in the future).

4

SUSTAINABLE TOURISM AND INTERNATIONAL ACTION

> "We are made for cooperation, like feet, like hands, like eyelids, like the rows of the upper and lower teeth. To act against one another then is contrary to Nature, and it is acting against one another to be vexed and turn away."
>
> —*Marcus Aurelius*

Basically, 'Sustainable' implies permanence. This connotes an integrated act in the environment, the "optimum" use of the resources, the involvement of the local population, the preservation and improvement of the surroundings, all of which allow a sustainable and therefore, lasting process as against the popular concept of the maximum use of space and time. But some tourist activities are not sustainable, and, therefore, scientific approach for sustainable development of tourism should be evolved which conserve and not consume the environment, establishing tourism environment capability. Such a development has to explore the relationship between the natural resources and the visitor community, with special regard to its conservation through sensitive planning and management.

Sustainable tourism was defined as the management of tourism resources in such a way that fulfill economic, social and aesthetic needs while maintaining cultural integrity, essential ecological processes, biological diversity and life support systems. In the words of Inskeep (1991) continuous maintenance of environmental resources and cultural integrity while still bringing equitably distributed socio-economic benefits of tourism to residents of the area is the essence of sustainable tourism development. According to the WTO (1993) 'Sustainability' is a more powerful concept of defining an appropriate approach to tourism development. It encompasses the requirements of all forms of tourism, from individuals travelling to the most sensitive environments to large groups visiting resort destination. Sustainable tourism development is development that has been carefully planned and is carefully managed. It is the antithesis of tourism that has developed for short run gains with the expectation that they will have a product life cycle declining after some years of fashion. Because of the pressure on the world's resources, it is the only sensible approach. The most successful tourism development of the future will be sustainable that is they will not over consume the resources used to attract tourists. Sustainability is generally taken to mean the existence of the ecological conditions necessary 'to support human life at a specified level of well being through future generations (Lele 1991).

This involves, according to Beaumont et al (1993): not using non-renewable resources faster than renewable substitutes can be found for them; not using renewable resources faster than they can be replenished; and not releasing pollutants faster than the biosphere can process them to be harmless and safe.

In the Words of Harris and Leper (1995) the combined term, sustainable development, can therefore be said to refer to a form of managed economic growth that occurs within the context of sound environmental stewardship. The goal of such stewardship being to pass on to future generations a stock of natural resources no less in quality or quantity (and preferably more) than that inherited by the current generation. This view of the concept of sustainable development is reflected in the most widely cited definition of the term, taken from the World Commission on Environment and Development (1987) report. In this document sustainable development is defined as 'development that meets the needs of the present without compromising the ability of future generations to meet their own needs'.

According to Manning (1996), a concept fundamental to the management of sustainable tourism is carrying capacity. It is founded on the experience of pastoral agriculture where it was observed that a pasture could support in perpetuity a particular number of cattle. If this threshold was exceeded, the supporting system was damaged, often to the point where it could no longer support grazing at all. In its simplest form, carrying capacity measures what level of use is sustainable. But originally it dealt with only one product-the number of cattle which could be fed by one pasture. In tourism, carrying capacity is much more complex, because a variety of products and services must come from the same environment.

The environment becomes the supply side to support tourism and other types of economic activities, while the demand side of the ecosphere model is driven by human numbers. Population and consumption demands include such things as food shelter, security, education, culture and recreation. This wider approach helps planners to better focus on achieving optional results in the development process. Since the 1992 Earth Summit, the concept of sustainable development has been placed firmly on the global agenda. It calls for a fundamental reorientation in the way we do business, in order to place the environment at the key centre of the decision making process for governments and their regional authorities, for communities, for environmental groups, and for business and industry.

First, it is significant to note that in this field, the efforts of WTO are appreciable. WTO is developing the European Union's Blue Flag standard for coastal quality as a model for application worldwide. In addition, it has produced a guide book to help local planners develop appropriate planning mechanisms and manage tourism effectively. In the field of accommodation International Hotel Association (IHA) assist hoteliers to reconcile environmental issues with competitive pressures through the production of guidelines and information on environmental auditing from time to time. It imposes self-regulation and avoid government regulation. It promotes the financial benefits of integrating environmental measures in hotels at the construction stage. IHA has developed and promoted Twelve Environmental Resolutions for the Hotel Industry (based on WTC's Recommended Environmental Guidelines) and hosts the Annual International Hotels Association Environment Award (sponsored by American Express International). It has also prepared a policy paper on tourism and the environment with the European Tourism Action Group (ETAG), study of environmentally sound design and siting of hotels (with UNEP and WTO), and a guide to environmental auditing of small and medium sized hotels.

International Hotels Environment Initiative (IHEI) is another important organisation of 11 international hotel companies to guide the development of the programme and to foster the continual upgrading of environmental performance in the hotel industry worldwide. American Society of Travel Agents (ASTA) environment Committee is also developing programmes for members dealing with adventure travel and its relation to ecotourism. It has promoted environmentally compatible forms of travel and ensure that endangered and over-stressed travel areas are preserved for the enjoyment of future generations. ASTA's 'Guidelines for Responsible Environmental Travel' have been issued to millions of travellers, operators, and destinations. In addition, members subscribe to an environmental code as it has established the Annual ASTA/ Smithsonian Magaxine Award for environmental excellence in the Travel and Tourism industry. An international environmental seminar titled 'Protecting the Environment: Tourism Responsibility and Profitability' was organised in India in 1994 in co-operation with the Indian Government.

It is likely to be repeated in other areas of the World in near future. Australian Tourism Industry Association (ATIA) is a representative association for the Travel & Tourism industry in Australia concerned with all aspects of tourism development in public and private sectors. It has developed environmental Policy to conserve and protect Australia's unique environment as the essential basis for the long-term success of the tourism industry. ATIA has developed and promoted the 'Code of Environmental Practice for the Tourism Industry'. As a part of the Prime Minister's Tourism Working Group, it participates in programmes on issues which may influence tourism development. International Chamber of Commerce (ICC) also helps Travel and Tourism businesses around the world and improve its environmental performance. It produced the Business Charter for Sustainable Development in 1991 which is the basis for many other codes of conduct and recently (1993) established the World Industry Council for the Environment (WICE) to advise governments on environmental issues as they affect business and promote sound environmental management in companies. International Air Transport Association's (IATA) Environmental Task Force (ETAF) has been concentrating on communicating the role of civil aviation in bringing about environmental protection tourist transit visitors over the last 20 years. ETAF's priorities in 1993 were to work toward minimixing unnecessary and impractical environmental restriction, to encourage fleet renewal and further reduction in airlines' environmental impacts, and to review the strategic responses required to meet the environmental challenges of the coming decade. International Federation of Tour Operators (IFTO) has established methods of assessing the impacts of tourism on the environment and guidelines for sustainable development. IFTO's regular meetings with national and regional governments, hoteliers and local tourist handling agents are used to promote environmentally sensitive policies for tourism development.

In 1992, IFTO obtained funding from the European Community and the Spanish Government for the development of models and methodologies for sustainable tourism under ECOMOST Project. This work had started in Mallorca and tested in Rhodes during 1993. From 1994, IFTO, with its partners, has been explaining how these models and methodologies can be put into practice in all resort areas, both in the European Community and Worldwide. IFTO will continue to promote environmental awareness amongst public and private sectors of the tourism industry as well as tourists. The largest tour operators in

Europe, TUI and Thomson both of which are members of IFTO, are very active in the environmental field, improving environmental performance as well as printing environmental information in all of their brochures.

International Union for the Conservation of Nature—(IUCN) has continued to develop its Environmental Law programme. In 1993, through the environmental law development component of the 'Programme, the final version draft of the International Covenant on Environment and Development was completed. IUCN provides advice and technical legal assistance to the governments of developing countries on request; publishes papers on relevant issues and sponsors regional conferences. In 1992, IUCN hosted the Fourth World Congress on National Parks and Protected Areas which produced the Caracas Declaration and an action plan entitled 'Parks for Life'. The third working group met to discuss the Draft Covenant for Environmental Conservation and Sustainable Natural Resources, including the obligations laid out in AGENDA 21 and the Rio Declaration. In collaboration with the International Council on Environmental Law (ICEL) and WTTC, IUCN held a meeting of senior legal experts on the 'Protection of Cultural and Natural Heritage in Times of Armed Conflict'. United Nations Environment Programme has a Industry and Environment Programme Activity Centre (UNEP IE/PAC). UN body responsible for environmental issues and representing the interests of the international community. It provides a platform to bring industry, government and NGOs together to work towards environmentally sound forms of industrial development. To this end, UNEP IE/PAC seeks to help formulate policies and strategies for sustainable industrial and tourism development, to facilitate their improvement and to stimulate the exchange of information. Its Key Activities/Achievements is to prepare technical reports, publications, workshops, seminars and forums, training and demonstration projects. In collaboration with other international associations, it developed AGENDA 21 programmes to promote environmentally sound activities industry wide.

Recent activities include a technical report on 'The Development of National Parks and Protected Areas for Tourism', a joint programme with UNESCO and WTO on tourism and the environment in world heritage sites, and publication of an issue on 'Sustainable Tourism Development' of the Industry and Environment review. World Travel and Tourism Council (WTTC) is a global coalition of chief executive officers from all sectors of Travel and Tourism, including transportation, accommodation, catering, recreational/cultural, and travel service activities.

It ensures that national and international policies appropriately reflect the scale and importance of the Travel and Tourism industry and, through the Environment Research Centre, to promote environmentally compatible growth in the industry. Based on its business Charter for Sustainable Development, it developed and promoted Environmental Guidelines for Travel and Tourism companies.

In collaboration with the International Council on Environmental Law (ICEL) and- IUCN it held a meeting of senior legal experts on the Protection of Cultural and Natural Heritage in times of armed conflict. It developed research into the contribution of Travel and Tourism to the economy and produced a comprehensive report. It launched a research programme on the perception of Travel and Tourism in the world economy. It campaigns to improve tourism infrastructure globally and eliminate barriers to travel.

WTTC will increase its efforts to promote environmentally compatible growth on the basis of management commitment, research and enlightened regulation.

Pacific Asia Travel Association (PATA) has launched a new PATA award scheme, called 'Green Leaf. It designed to encourage good environmental behaviour by all suppliers of Travel and Tourism products and services as well as the use of environmental purchase criteria by consumers. This programme is based on PATA's 'Code for Environmentally Responsible Tourism' (CERT), promulgated in 1992 and the details of PATA's Code for Environmentally Responsible Tourism is as follows:

- ADOPT the necessary practices to conserve the environment, including the use of renewable resources in a sustainable manner and the conservation of non-renewable resources;
- CONTRIBUTE to the conservation of any habitat of flora and fauna, and of any site whether natural or cultural, which may be affected by tourism;
- ENCOURAGE relevant authorities to identify areas worthy of conservation and to determine the level of development, if any, which would ensure those areas are conserved;
- ENSURE that environmental assessment becomes an integral step in the consideration of any site for a tourism project;
- COMPLY with all international, conventions in relation to the environment;

- COMPLY with all national, state, and local laws in relation to the environment;
- ENCOURAGE those involved in tourism comply with local, regional, and national planning policies and to participate in the planning process;
- PROVIDE the opportunity for the wider community to take part in discussions and consultations on tourism planning issues in so far as they affect the tourism industry and the community;
- ACKNOWLEDGE responsibility for the environmental impacts of all tourism related projects and activities and undertake all necessary responsible, remedial, and corrective actions;
- ENCOURAGE regular environmental audits of practices throughout the tourism industry and encourage necessary changes to those practices;
- FOSTER environmentally responsible practices, including waste management, recycling, and energy use;
- FOSTER, in both management and staff of all tourism-related projects and activities, an awareness of environmental and conservation principles;
- SUPPORT the inclusion of professional conservation principles in tourism education, training, and planning;
- ENCOURAGE an understanding by all those involved in tourism of each community's customs, cultural values, beliefs and traditions, and how they relate to the environment;

- ENHANCE the appreciation and understanding by tourists of the environment through the provision of accurate information and appropriate interpretation; and
- ESTABLISH detailed environmental policies and/ or guidelines for the various sectors of the tourism industry.

Further, the International Civil Aviation Environment organisation's Committee on Aviation Environmental Protection (CAEP) substantially revised its work programme in 1992 to place particular emphasis on determining the contribution of engine emission to problems in the upper atmosphere and to identify appropriate solutions to these problems. Its aim and objective is to develop and promote environmentally responsible practices within the air transport industry in cooperation with other international bodies. ICAO is additionally concerned with establishing noise and emission standards for aircraft. ICAO has responsibility for the development of international guidelines and environmental standards for aircraft operations.

In 1990, it developed a worldwide policy Aviation Environmental Protection-Whose work programme was substantially revised in 1992 to give increased—emphasis to the impact of civil aviation on the upper atmosphere. Lufthansa, German Airlines, has developed a range of self-regulatory initiatives to minimise the impacts of its operations on the environment, employing the latest technology while instilling a sense of environmental responsibility among all personnel.

The Chairman of the Executive Board, stated that "acceptance of responsibility for the environment is as much a part of the company's objectives as maintaining good customer relations or being competitive in the market". Lufthansa has frequently taken action in specific areas well ahead of regulatory requirements: For example, the company has invested in a younger fleet to reduce noise and gaseous pollutants. The average age of the Lufthansa fleet is now less than six years, making it one of the world's youngest. The company has also invested in research to replace environmentally hazardous techniques or substances. Some companies, such as British Airways, run schemes to award environmental achievements within the company.

Thailand-based Siam City Hotels & Resorts holds competitions for environmental ideas from employees, for example, a contest for 'green cartoons'. Qantas, for example, shows in-flight videos, developed with the co-operation of World Wide Fund for Nature (WWF), highlighting the problems generated by purchasing souvenirs made from the hides, tusks, horns and shells of endangered species of animals. Thomson Tour Operators has put environmental information into brouchures and trained representatives at resorts in using environmentally sound products. East Japan Railway Company has been striving to maintain a pleasant environment along its routes. Since 1992, 30,000 seedlings a year have been planted by company members and people living alongside the company's railways.

British Airways Holidays has produced environmental destination guides for Thailand, Kenya and the Caribbean and offers customers the opportunity to donate, with a supporting donation from the company, to conservation projects endorsed by IUCN. Travel & Tourism companies can also play an important role in conserving resources through communication and education initiatives. Japan Travel Bureau, Japan's leading tour operator, organized a tour of Malaysia's tropical rain forest to show the damage that had been done and to raise support for a reforestation scheme. American Airlines encourages corporate staff and family involvement in the enhancement of the environment. KLM Royal Dutch Airlines is reducing the number of private cars driving to Schipol airport by developing more efficient public transport. East Japan Railway company has encouraged passengers *to* support its recycling programme by placing separate bins for bottles and cans, newspapers and magazines, and other waste in stations.

This has made it possible to reduce the amount of waste produced each year by roughly half. Asilomar State Beach and Conference Grounds in the USA have replanted thousands of native dune species, and presented more than 1,200 interpretive programmes to over 40,000 clients emphasizing the importance of preserving local flora and fauna. Thus, the India, despite known for sustainable development approach right from the time of the Mauryas, when were introduced do's and don'ts for *Abhiyaranyas* (Parks), could not plan and control natural resources of the country systematically.

We frame rules and regulations for sustainable development of tourist places but could not implement respective guidelines and development evaluation standards. Goa is perhaps the only state which is highly conscious of the need to maintain and preserve nature, ecology and Environment protection act, 1986, enforced by the Union Ministry of Environment and Forests through its notification issued in February, 1991. The development needs to be monitored carefully lest they are in danger of environment damage that is irreversible. The Konkan railway project in the Western Ghats is on completion and needs precautionary measures before it got delayed. Western Ghats are unique both naturally and geologically. The Ghats are the system of land elevation, hills, mountains, plateaus and dotted with beautiful sea beaches from Bombay to Kanyakumari. Bombay is the entry point of foreign tourist arrivals. But, after economic liberalisation in 1991, the occupancy rate of accommodation units increased and Bombay city has started to cater more number of tourists than ever.

Exceeding pressures of increased commercial units and increased migration of people, Mumbai has deteriorated both its land and coasts due to over exploitation of natural resources. A number of proposals have been made for the protection of flora and fauna and restoration of lakes, fountains and streams in the Himalaya. But it is noticed that a fairly large number of valleys, meadows, slopes, glaciers and forests are loosing their existence, serenity and culture day by day as mass influx of visitors have not only created the problem of carrying capacity but increased the possibilities of social and visual pollution and ruthless duploitation. HIMTAB organises Mountain Tourism meets inside of Hotel Complexes is required to take subject experts to such destinations which have been severely affected by man-made and physical onslauguts.

There is lack of co-ordination with local people as we do not find active participation of *Gram-Pradhans* and local Social Workers in the planning and management of tourist places. Development parametres and tourism measurement methods should be applied on destination wise not for the entire Himalaya as a whole. The lakes of India, require careful planning from all concerned. The role of Planning Commission is commendable as it has recommended that the National Lake Conservation Plan (NLCP) be considered a centrally sponsored scheme in the ninth plan, with all the funds being provided by the centre. The eleven lakes out of twenty one lakes covered for this purpose are Dal (J&K), Sukhna (Chandigarh), Sagar and Bhoj (M.P.), Nainital (U.K.), Kodai Kanal, Ooty (Tamil Nadu), Rabindra Sagar (West Bengal), Powai (Maharashtra), Udaipur lakes (Rajasthan) and Hussain Sagar (Andhra Pradesh). The Andhra Government is also planning to entrust private parties with the beautification of Hussain Sagar lake and developing it as a tourist spot. India's historic monuments and cultural sites are internationally known. But most of the architecturally rich centres are not renovated because of lack of funds. Environmental degradation, industrial pollution and illegal encroachments have taken their toll where efforts have been made at conservation the results have been crude and insenstive.

However, the efforts of Delhi Government to hand over some historical monuments here for preservation and upkeep to business houses is appreciable. The Rajasthan Government has also taken initiative in this field as the Archaeological Survey of India probably did not pay more attention on historic buildings richly carved by marvels. But one factor which has had a lasting impact on the process of conservation is the lack of Co-ordination between the Ministry of Tourism and the Ministry of Culture. While the former still adheres to the old ASI approach, the Ministry of Tourism has adopted a revenue generating approach, But things are changing now for the better.

For the first time, a sub committee has been included in the Ninth Five Year Plan, which is to devise ways of amalgamating tourism and culture. Besides, pressure by the serious minded architects and builders is also being built for a greater public accountability for the kind of work that is being done for the preservation of various structures. The private sector in India has pioneered some of our most creative environmentally sustainable ventures especially in Kerala, Tamil Nadu and Karnataka. The Taj Group of Hotels has recently implemented a comprehensive environmental programme within its chain of hotels and produces 'Eco Taj', an impressive/environmental magazine for the staff. To offer responsible Tours and soft travel under the banner of 'Small' is beautiful' one of such venture is Kolam (based in Chennai) based Kolam Responsible Tour Agency.

It attempts to value caucious and qualitative in contrast to the price conscious and quantitative mass tourism'. Improving quality has become the single most important issue facing most of the developed and environmental friendly tourism sectors. It is also vital for the countries new and emerging tourist destinations, which have a chance to implement quality standards. Quality in the newly opened tourism destinations can be achieved if the issue is tackled from the outset, starting with physical planning, the design of infrastructure, architecture and ecology.

The car-free Austrian ski resort of Lech emerged as an example of sustainable destination where quality environmental value like top priority over mass development and big numbers on the arrival sheet were the main issues of tourism promotion. Residents of Lech have voted against nosting the world ski Championships and against new development, in favour of maintaining and caring for what already exists.

The close relationship between tourism and the environment and the importance of environmental planning and sustainable tourism development planning are becoming increasingly recognised.

The Manila Declaration (1980) of the World Tourism Organisation (WTO), the most comprehensive international statement adopted on the goals of modern tourism, emphasises the importance of both natural and cultural resources in tourism and the need for conservation of these resources for the benefit of both tourism and residents of the tourism area. Following on from the Manila Declaration, the Joint Declaration of the WTO and United Nations Environment Programme (UNEP), which formalised inter-agency coordination on tourism and the environment, states:

> "The protection, enhancement and improvement of the various components of man's environment are among the fundamental conditions for the harmonious development of tourism. Similarly, rational management of tourism may contribute to a large extent to protecting and developing the physical environment and the cultural heritage, as well as improving the quality of life".

The importance of national and regional tourism planning as a conservation and sustainable development technique was expressed at a WTO/UNEP Environmental Workshop in 1983 as follows:

> "Regional planning provides probably the best opportunity for achieving environmental protection goals through the use of zoning strategies. Thus zoning strategies and regulations can be used to encourage the concentration in some areas and/or dispersion in other areas of tourist activity so the extreme pressures are restricted to resilient environments and fragile environments can be given the most rigid protection measures, e.g. Cot Donana, in Spain. In this manner, nature conservation interests can be accorded their

appropriate priority where it is the prime land use designation...."

Appropriate relationships between tourism and the natural and socio-cultural environments, which places responsibilities on both the tourist-receiving countries and the tourists themselves, were further specified by the WTO in 1985 during its Sixth General Assembly through its adoption of the Tourism Bill of Rights and Tourist Code.

This statement contained the following provisions:

- In the interest of present and future generations, (States should) protect the tourist environment which, being at once human, natural, social and cultural, is the legacy of all mankind....
- The populations constituting host communities in places of transit and stay are entitled to free access to their own tourism resources...
- They are also entitled to expect from tourists, understanding of the respect for their customs, religions and other elements of their cultures which are part of human heritage.
- To facilitate such understanding and respect, the dissemination of appropriate information should be encouraged on:
    - (i) the customs of host communities, their traditional and religious practices, local taboos and sacred sites and shrines, which must be respected;
    - (ii) their artistic, archaeological and cultural treasures, which must be preserved; and
    - (iii) wildlife and other natural resources, which must be protected.

- Tourists should, by their behaviour, foster understanding and friendly relations among peoples, at both the national and international levels, and thus contribute to lasting peace.
- At places of transit and stay, tourists must respect the established political, social, moral and religious order and comply with legislation and regulations in force. In these places, tourists must also:
    - (i) show the greatest understanding for the customs, beliefs and behaviour of the host communities and the greatest respect for their natural and cultural heritage...; and
    - (ii) refrain from exploiting others.....

Prior to the adoption of the Tourism Bill of Rights and Tourist Code by the WTO, WTO and the UNEP had held an earlier joint workshop in 1983 on the Environmental Aspects of Tourism. Among other conclusions reached by the Workshop participants, several statements touched on the social-cultural problems introduced by mass tourism:

- When tourists enter the host country, they do not just bring their purchasing power... they also, and above all, bring a different type of society which profoundly transforms local social habits by removing and upsetting the basic and long-established values and patterns of behaviour of the host population.
- Tourism is indeed, therefore, a 'total social event' which leads to structural changes in all sectors of society and which becomes generalised by

progressively being extended to all regions of the globe.

- During the tourist season, the resident population not only has to accept the effects of overcrowding, which do not exist for the remainder of the year, but they must often completely modify their way of life (increased work rhythm, dual activity, etc.) and live in close contact with a different type of population, mainly urban, who are there simply for leisure. However, this 'coexistence' is not always easy and often leads to social tension, xenophobia, particularly noticeable in very populous tourist areas or where the population, for psychological, cultural or social reasons, is not ready to be submitted to the 'the tourist invasion'.

Further, the Hague Declaration on Tourism, adopted at the Inter-Parliamentary Conference on Tourism (organised jointly by the Inter-Parliamentary Union and the WTO) in 1989 set forth several principles for development of tourism, including emphasising the importance of integrated planning of tourism. This declaration also pointed the essential relationship of the environment and tourism, as follows (WTO 1989): "An unspoilt natural, cultural and human environment is a fundamental condition for the development of tourism. Moreover, rational management of tourism may contribute significantly to the protection and development of the physical environment and the cultural heritage, as well as to improving the quality of life".

Osaka Tourism Forum

The importance of environment was also recognised in the Osaka Tourism net. High-ranking officials and tourism ministers from 96 countries called for preservation of the natural environment and increased international co-operation during the Osaka World Tourist Forum, 94. The declaration, the first of its kind since the Manila Declaration of 1980, calls on tourists and the tourism industry to share the responsibility for protecting the environment and respecting cultural values.

The notable features of the Osaka Tourism Declaration were as follows:

- tourism is the greatest producer of world gross domestic product and employment, accounting for one-tenth of each.
- the growth of international tourism contributes to the promotion of mutual understanding among countries and peoples.
- tourism is an effective means of income redistribution between countries and thus contributes to a more balanced development of world economies.
- tourism is essentially an act of being in touch with, appreciating and learning from bountiful nature and foreign societies and cultures. In that regard, tourists should possess humility and respectfulness in their journeys.
- the destruction of traditional cultures and lifestyles and exploitation of vulnerable groups caused by tourism development can lead to serious consequences and must be avoided. Tourists must also bear responsibility for discreet and desirable behaviour to avoid negatively influencing local society.

- tourism should never be the destroyer, rather, it should be the protector. If the tourism industry and tourists share responsibility for conservation of the environment and cultural heritage, it becomes possible to preserve their value and at the same time use them as tourism resources.
- governments need to have a greater awareness of the crucial role tourism plays in the formulation of policy and should formulate policies with an emphasis on tourism.

But in recent years it is noticed that there has been little progress since the ambitious Rio Summit which was considered the blueprint for sustainable development. This situation at present is alarming: more than 50,000 square miles of forests are being stripped of their green cover every day, green house gases emission is at an all time high, and the number of people living on less than a dollar per day has risen to above 1.1 billion. Forest fires have become more common; around 200,000 hectares of Mediterranean forests are destroyed each year by fire. Over 500 Mediterranean plant species are threatened with extinction. The U.S. along with China, Japan, Indonesia, Russia, Germany, Brazil and India have 56 per cent of the world's population and 53 per cent of its forest cover.

But under no circumstances can all these countries be held equally responsible for the environment as they are in the various stages of development. In fact, it becomes incumbent upon the more industrialised countries and indeed funding agencies like the World Bank to ensure that aid to the developing World does not go to projects which have the potential to destroy natural ecosystems. Economic growth in any nation cannot be at the cost of sustainable development. Tourism industry, covers diverse activities such as transport, accommodation, entertainment, catering, handicrafts and souvenirs among many others. Some may have severe negative impacts on visiting destinations and population in the absence of proper checks and balances.

Tourism development puts pressure on all local resources; tourists consume energy, water, food and other raw materials, some of which may be in short supply locally. Tourists now go everywhere and on account of this, some of the destinations have come up very recently, some have achieved balanced position in Tourism business and a few of them have reached saturation Point. Developing countries like India, where tourism as a business activity is a recent happening, have already started to realise repercussions at a number of tourist places. India receives much smaller number of tourists in comparison to some other countries. But due to haphazard development, some tourism destinations have lost their naturality and are likely to become the centres of garbage and litter very soon. 2.3 million foreign tourists is a much smaller number to cause great deal of damage who come into this vast country of 950 million people, but the much larger number of domestic tourists and pilgrims cause greater damage. According to a -rough estimate of the Ministry of Tourism, Govt. of India the domestic tourists today account to about 135 million. Besides this, there are visitors to special events like Kumbh Mela where lakhs of people congregate at one place and take a holy dip. We cannot prevent them to visit sacred holy places as it is linked to their religious sentiments. It is estimated that every year Indians are paying Rs. 34,000 crore due to the effects of massive environmental degradation which will eventually threaten our future generations. Water and air pollution along impose a health cost of Rs. 24,500 crore every year The economic loss due to environmental degradation has been grossly understaimated due to lack of adequate data. Ahmedabad, Mumbai, Kolkata, Delhi, Kanpur and Nagpur, the major centres of business centres, have three times more suspended particulate matter than prescribed by the World Health Organisation (WHO). Carbon Monoxide emissions in many cities are 50 times higher than the WHO standards.

The Himalaya in Danger

The nightly Himalaya spread in a total length of 2400 km., measured along the arc; the width varies from 325 to 425 km. The actual Himalayan range commences at Naga Parbat (8126 m) in the north-west, passes through Pakistan, Kashmir, Himachal Pradesh, and ends at Namche Barwa (7825 m) in the east (Singh 1992). Glaciers in Himalaya are receding rapidly. Heaps of garbage are increasing day by day either in Rohtang Pass, Zoiila or Everest. With the expansion of urbanisation, the Himalaya has started to receive increased number of visitors. Increased pressure of visitors on mountain tourism has been identified by a few mountain tourism scholars (Sinnhuber 1982; Singh 1982; Messerli 1982; Groetzbach 1984; Brugger et at, 1984, Kaur 1985; Jandari 1986; Lichtenberger 1988; Price 1992; Singh et al 1992, Shrestha 1995). The situation in the Himalaya needs careful monitoring so that unnecessary human interference may not cause serious problem. Noted environmentalists Sunderlal Bahuguna (1996), recently stressed the need for banning human movements in the form of trekking and mountaineering on glaciers. Glaciers, along with forest, are the permanent storehouse, of water in the Himalaya and must be protected at all costs. The Govt. of India has recently made the area accessible for foreign tourists and it has further increased the overall number of international trekkers and nature lovers. The increased number of visitors and sellers of daily needed items have further made the area crowed. The recession of the glaciers is causing a high level of ecological stress in the Himalayan region, according to a study by the Glaciological Survey of India.

The Himalaya constitute one of the most important glacier systems in the world, covering a vast area. Nearly 15000 glaciers exist in the Himalaya and are an important source of fresh water of North India's perennial rivers.

Recently a snow-capped peak is noticed slided in Badrinath area in Uttarakhand. Pindari Glacier has also receded to a great magnitude. The Gangotri Glacier, in the Garhwal Himalaya, has been shrinking at an alarming rate and had receded at the rate of 7.31 metres annually during the last century, 18 metres a year until 1990 and of more than 20 metres per year after 1990. Over the last 50 years, the Gangotri Glacier has receded by 600 metres. Due to recession of glaciers, the unique plant wealth of the high altitude meadows in the Himalaya is also being affected. Some of the flowers locally knows Brahma Kamal, Barmoola, Laljari, Neelkanthi, and Ratanjot—all medicinal and aromatic plants, are found in these meadows. Relentless killing of wild flowers has caused irreparable loss to the flowering species. As a result, many of them have vanished from forests and some will disappear in near future. A fairly large number of wild flower species are now on the verge of permanent extinction.

A recent report published by the United Nations Environment Programme (UNEP) contains some bombshells as how man has maimed biodiversity. According to the report, 4000 plant species, most of them flowering plants, are currently threatened with extinction. During forthcoming decades, the tropical forests are likely to loose a sizable chunk of their flowering plant species. The Himalaya is also known for *a* variety of wild flowers. Out of 2,80,000 tree species (most of them flowering species), I 5,000 flowering tree species are found in the Himalaya. Kullu, Manali, Kangra, Shimla, Kinnaur, Kumaun, Garhwal, J & K, Darjeeling etc. have lost much of their wild charms.

The tourist places like Shimla, Kufri, Naldehra, Kasauli, Chail and Solan which were at one time famous wild bloom spots are loosing their natural set-up as wild flowers have dramatically vanished from the valleys of the State. One of the structures at Kufri near Shimla was named as Wild Flower Hall. Now neither wild flowers nor the famous structure exist. Indiscreet cutting of trees are turning these forests into brown deserts and have led to hill erosion. Nainital is also no longer a green valley. The increasing influx of tourists has led to a host of problems.

The problems of this town have turned out to be more acute because of its geographical limitations, concentration of building activity and tourist traffic in and around the natural lake. Excessive construction and a gradual depletion of the green cover, along with intensified demographic pressure on its limited resources has badly mutilated this once beautiful destination of tourists. This town has a population of 32,000. But during the peak tourist season, the figure rises to two lakh. As per forest department sources, between 1950 and 1975, approximately 40,000 trees were felled down in the town for different purposes, mainly for construction of hotel buildings.

A pastoral village Manali, with 650 households, was suddenly overwhelmed by outsiders emerging from Indian metropolises and from the West. The planned area increased from 47 to 194 hectares within the span of a decade. On account of political movement in U.P. hills, and problem of terrorism in J & K, tourist traffic to Manali had increased fourfold during the last seven years. To check the mushrooming growth of commercial units, a height restriction of 33 feet has been in place for about three years, but four storeyed hotels are a common sight.

For the last 3 years, there has been a ban on construction of houses and hotels within 50 metres and 100 metres of the Beas river bank at different locations. But surprisingly, around fifty and twenty new hotels came up in 1995 and 1996 respectively. In Mussoorie, its inherent beauty has been spoilt because of the garbage and filth left behind by increased number of visitors. According to. Self-Help Environment Programme (SHEP), due to excessive presence of non-biodegradable substances in the area, a variety of plants like moss are dying and the entire hydrological regime of Mussoorie has been altered leading to the drying of water channels. Similar problems have been noticed in the higher Himalaya where people go for mountaineering. As the Monsoon season comes to an end, thousands of our young people visit the Himalaya. We notice maximum number of trekkers to Gangotri, Pindari Glacier, Amarnath, Rohtang Pass and Sikkim Himalaya, besides millions of tourists and pilgrims to hill stations and religious shrines respectively. An environmental time bomb is ticking beneath the simmering waters of the world famous Dal Lake in Srinagar, Kashmir, and environmentalists fear that unless immediate steps are taken the lake would disappear very soon. Once a star tourist attraction with its famed *Shikaras,* the lake appears to be facing a slow death due to increasing encroachment along its banks, dumping of wastes, mechanical deweeding and sluggish water movement. The lake has shrunk from 48 sq.kms, in 1947 to mere 12 sq.kms. or less today.

The Comptroller and Auditor General of India (CAG), which had tabled the report on Dal Lake in 1997 in the state legislature said that human interference by way of settlement on the lake shores, construction of embankments within the lake, increase in number of house-boats for tourists, and denudation of the catchment area have been the cause of shrinkage and pollution of the lake. The area of the lake shrink from 24 sq.kms. in 1962 to 15 sq.kms. in 1982. The condition of Ladakh is also not satisfactory. M.S. Kohli, former President of Indian Mountaineering Federation, opines when he first visited Ladakh on an expedition to Saser Kangri in 1956 not many from the outside world had visited the area. The age-old local habits and customs of the Ladakh were intact, and this in itself was a rewarding experience. At each village they were invited by the local people to their houses with folded hands. But the old culture and hospitality has finished.

By opening Ladakh for tourists, many of the historic monasteries have been stripped. In the words of the first Union Minister for Tourism and Civil Aviation, Govt. of India, Karan Singh, "The monasteries have just been stripped because if a person is sitting in a monastery for 500 years in a tradition and a tourist comes and offers US $ 100 for some work of art: $ 100 may be a paltry sum for the tourist but for a poor person who is sitting in a monastery, $ 100 is something. And we know that they are very convinced about reincarnation. Therefore, a large number of tank has and other art treasures have disappeared." Increased number of Mountaineering expeditions have eroded the peaks of faith of the Himalaya since 1980. In case of the Mount Everest two people climbed the submit in 1970, ten in 1980 but there were 72 who reached the top in 1990. But the increase in the number of successful climbers has been matched by an equal rise in mortality figures. There were only 44 death between 1921 and 1970 but in 1992, 115 died. Today, according to Ahluwalia (1997) the number of deaths per annum has crossed the 150 mark. Santosh Yadav, the Indian Woman mountaineer, who enjoys the distinction of having climbed Everest twice, reminisces about a particular difficult night at South Col in 1993, "I spent the night resting my head against a rock which was jutting into the tent. Imagine my horror when I woke up in the morning to find it was not a rock but a dead body." Nepal Mountaineering Association has attempted to clean the Himalaya.

National Parks and Sanctuaries

Though 9.2 per cent of country's land falls in the category of protected area which includes 85 National Parks with 1.08%, 446 Sanctuaries with 3.43%, and 531 protected areas with 4.5% of the area; visitors and local population pressure, unsavoury conflicts among NGOs over human and animal rights, spread of industrial interests into protected areas and a major spurt in poaching activities with rhino horn and tiger bones fetching thousands of dollars in the international markets are some of outstanding issues that threaten our national parks and genetic wealth they hold. However, the renotification of protected sanctuaries like Darlaghat in Himachal and Narayan Sarovar in Gujarat to set up cement factories and other industries causes worry. The construction of a fishing jetty at Bhitarkanika could sound the death-knell of Olive Ridley turtles that come to breed every year on the undisturbed shores of the Orissa coast. In Rajasthan efforts are going on to extend the dolomite mining work even it falls in protected areas like the Sariska Tiger Reserve. A third of the Melaghat National Park is being denotified in the guise of reducing human and wildlife conflict.

The Indian Institute of Public Opinion study showed that in 1989, 56 per cent of the national parks and 72 per cent of the sanctuaries surveyed had population within their boundaries. Bansda in Gujarat had a density of 56 persons per hectare. The growing human population is putting tremendous pressure on protected areas by increasing the demands for fuelwood, fodder and other forest produce.

Whereas a large number of national parks and sanctuaries without any funds or means for proper protection and conservation cannot be supported. Care has to be taken to obtain a balance, and conservation of core areas and endangered species of both flora and fauna have to be ensured. The Nilgiri bioreserve which spreads over the borders of Karnataka, Kerala and Tamil Nadu constitutes 15 per cent of India's total protected area also repeats the same story. The reserve shelters around 100 mammalian species, 550 species of birds and 30 reptilian ones-thus acquiring an unparalleled biological status that has led to its blatant plunder by the international wildlife trade cartel. A study conducted by Vatavaran, an NGO, revealed that the very animals which are supposed to be under total protection inside the reserve are being traded at its fringes. In Kerala, construction of roads have disturbed the wildlife of Periyar National Park.

The Kerala Forest Department's proposal to construct a network of roads within the famous Periyar Tiger Reserve, located at Thekkady in the Idukki district, may cause negative impacts on wildlife habitat. The department proposes to strengthen its patrolling and provided more protection to wildlife by constructing seven motorable roads of 138 kms. to canned various parts of the sanctuary with the existing approach roads. The five-year project, to be completed in phases, would link places lika Mavady, Mullakudy, Mullathode and Thannikudy-all situated within the thick evergreen forests. The blasting of granite for the first phase of the project linking Mavady and Thannikurdy had already begun. The sanctuary's delicate eco-system faces the danger of being destroyed by the construction activity. Remarkably, the road construction seemingly violates the forest management guidelines prescribed by the Union Ministry of Environment and Forests. The proposed roads would cut through areas with a high density of tigers and with the rising human pressure and cutting of trees during the construction, wildlife there could be greatly dislocated. The Gir lion reserve also does not feel safe. Noise and air pollution are making the survival of the lion increasingly difficult in the 1,412 sq. kms. protected territory of the Gir sanctuary. Disturbed by the increasing presence of man and affected by the pollution caused by vehicles passing through the five state highways crisscrossing the Gir, many lions are exiling themselves to the periphery of the jungle, often becoming easy targets for poachers and poisoning by villagers.

Many tourists come to Gir in their own vehicles. This is in addition to the numerous trucks owned by cement companies that pass through the Gir. Nobody can stop them if they intend to interfere in the reserve. Some visitors come to the Gir under the pretext of a pilgrimage, and leave behind a large number littered on the road, which are harmful to the animals. Cattle grazing along the boundary and inside the forest has increased in number, which explains that the lions have moved to the outskirts of the jungle.

Bandhavgarh, once known hunting ground of Maharaja of Rewa estate, is now a national park. Although a small park compared to parks like Kanha and Corbett, it boasts of an incredible variety of species of mammals, birds and reptiles. But today, Bandhavgarh has begun to realise discord between human beings and nature, resulting in the destruction of the latter. It is only because of the lack of knowledge and understanding on the part of the human beings. A check in the number of visitors to the park on any given day is required to be observed. It is necessary to determine the carrying capacity of the park.

In recent years, many camps and lodges have come up around the national parks, and contrary to popular belief, the interest of those who run the camps goes beyond just financial gains. The forest department will do well to take these organisations into confidence. The operators are ever ready to assist in enforcing a strict code of conduct within the park, for the very existence of these camps and lodges depends on a healthy and natural environment.

The Jim Corbett National Park, the first national park and tiger reserve of the country receives tremendous threat to its tigers from poachers. Under "Project Tiger" scheme launched in 1973, apart from 520.18 sq. kms. of the Corbett National Park the 301.18 sq. kms. of the Sonanadi Wildlife sanctuary and 496.54 sq. kms. of the reserve forest also became-part of the protected area. The Corbett Tiger Reserve is among the 23 such reserves in the country. The local people here say that most of the poaching cases go unreported unless an animal carcass is found or some persons arrested with animal parts.

According to sources here, most of the poaching is done in the peripheral divisions where the forest staff is engaged in routine work and not properly equipped. The forest officers have no magisterial powers and they do not have arms either. In the foothills of the central Himalaya near Hardwar, the Rajaji National Park has been facing the increased and continued biotic pressure on the forest area in and around the park. The *Gujjars,* a Muslim pastoral tribe, and their cattle have expanded to three times or more of their original number. With their buffaloes, cows, ponies and sheep, the *Gujjars* are causing depletion of the precious Sal forests. The effects are visible all over the park where the undergrowth is disappearing and trees are dying due to excessive lopping. In the eastern part of the country, the Kaziranga National Park, famous for one horn rhino, also faces the problem of poaching and hunting. It is estimated that a kilogram of rhino horn is priced at Rs. 25 to 30 lakhs in the international markets and the main demands for horns is from Taiwan, Hongkong, China, Thailand, Singapore and Yemen in the Middle-East. In Yemen it is used in dagger handles by the rich individuals. The Rhino Foundation, set up in 1994 with funding from some 90 tea garden companies, has played an important role in building awareness against poaching. A lot of rhinos are shot during the monsoons when they leave the security of the park to cross over to the high grounds of the tea gardens.

The US Fish and Wildlife Department is providing funds for follow up of the poaching cases. As direct incentives to the field staff, the Foundation has been distributing water filters to the forest camps and hunting boots, raincoats and warm sweaters to guards. However, the forest guards need training in use of rifles and the initiative has to come from the Government. They also need country boats, speed boats and elephants for patrolling inside the national park.

Plans to expand the protected area of the rhino territotry by 490 sq. kms. and ensure a corridor for their migration to the hills in the monsoons is providing difficult as local people are not allowing the government to acquire their lands. But if the rhino is to be saved and protected, there is urgent need to acquire some 430 sq. kms. at Burapahar where migrating rhinos run straight into the bullets of poachers. The 470 sq. kms. Manas National Park of Assam, a world heritage site, has become the home of armed Bodo militants and poacher gangs who have been felling trees and killing wildlife as well as foresters.

The World Wide Fund (WWF), as a part of its framework for regional cooperation in south Asia to generate a more realistic and focussed approach towards overall conservation programmes, has chalked out a Comprehensive Tiger Conservation Action Plan to strengthen ongoing efforts for protection of tigers through new and innovative initiatives. The strategy includes mobilisation of support for tiger conservation at political and policy making levels, generating grassroots support through local communities and a support mechanism by way of information collection and dissemination, education and awareness.

The strategy also emphasises the need to facilitate inter-governmental consultations to discuss trans boundary issues between India and Nepal and field level discussions on tiger conservation work in the region, in collaboration with Nepal and Bhutan. Further, effective campaign on illegal trade-"Don't buy trouble"-has been undertaken as an initiative under "WWF 2000 Living Planet Campaign," to address both supplier and consumer countries of animal parts.

During implementation, this strategy will be subjected

to continuous monitoring and periodic review and focus will be on the 12 Indian states which account for about 93 per cent of the country's tiger population. According to the WWF, total wild population of five sub-species of tigers is at present estimated to been between 4,600 and 7,200 and the sub-species found in the Indian subcontinent (India, Bangladesh, Nepal and Bhutan)-*panthera tigris*-constitutes the largest population of all surviving tiger subspecies. Significantly, the tiger population in India represents around 53 per cent of the global tiger population.

Certification for Sustainable Tourism

As a recent development, a growing number of tourism businesses are voluntarily participating in certification systems that grant a seal of approval to companies or destinations that demonstrate environmentally or socially sound practices. Not only do these labels serve as useful marketing tools, but they can motivate the industry to develop more environmentally-friendly products. They can also provide consumers with valuable information on sustainable tourism products, helping them to make more informed travel choices. The ultimate success of tourism certification as a conservation tool rests on whether or not it can set a trusted, reliable standard, and on the degree to which the industry and consumers worldwide demonstrate their support.

Basically, Tourism is a private sector activity, driven in large part by international hotel chains, tour companies and other businesses. The process of making tourism more sustainable requires careful planning at many levels and the participation of all potential stakeholders, particularly of local communities directly affected by tourism's presence. While the drive to adopt more sustainable practices is inherently complex, many in the tourism industry have already taken a number of positive steps toward becoming more environmentally and socially responsible.

A number of the world's larger tourism companies, from hotels to tour operators, are in the throes of restructuring their management and operations to reduce the consumption of water, energy and other resources, and to improve the management, handling and disposal of waste. Some companies are adopting the environmental management standard set out by the International Standards Organization, ISO 140001. In addition to saving money, these operational shifts are key to sustainability. Agenda 21 ranks the incorporation of environmental management principles as "among the highest corporate priorities and as a key determinant to sustainability."

Sustainable Coastal Tourism

No exaggeration, in the name of coastal tourism, Indian beaches are possibly the most attractive anywhere in the world. During the winter season when most of the western world, our tourism market, is suffering from sub-zero temperature and India's own northern and eastern regions are under a cold spell, the beaches of Goa, Mahabalipuram and Kovalam offer you unbelievably blue skies, excellent weather and miles upon miles of clear beaches and lapping waves. Indian beaches are rich in natural assets therefore their development needs to be monitored carefully lest they are in danger of environment damage that is irreversible. The increasing number of visitors to sea beaches have a great pressure on nature and this can be noticed at a number of coastal resorts of South India. Though tourism, in the region, except Goa, has not acquired large scale proportion but with the facility of charters to coastal tourism destinations and advent of Konkan Railway are likely to tilt the balance. It is therefore important to undertake an exhaustive environmental assessment study before we plan to promote any sea beach for fun, frolic and recreation. India has also opened Andaman, Nicobar and Lakshadweep islands for Coastal Tourism which are ecological far more fragile than rest of the country's sea beaches.

Keeping in view the nature of country's sea beaches the Ministry of Tourism, Govt. of India had set-up a sub-group committee in 1989 to review different issues related to beach tourism promotion (Kumar 1995). According to the Committee the following points may be taken into consideration before opening any coastal area for sea beach purpose.

- The beach and off-share water conditions must be of a sufficiently high quality.
- The beach must be of sufficient size in length and width to accommodate large numbers of people without congestion and crowding.
- The beach should have sufficient sand visually attractive in colour, fine in texture, pleasant in touch and generally clean from rocks, corals and debris.
- The beach should have gentle shelf into the water to allow safe entry to and exist from the surf.
- The resort should be attractive, more of rural setting which is conducive for leisure and relaxation than to have congested settings of urban centres.
- The overall environment should express a sense of uniqueness and a quality and character that set in apart from other competitive tourism destinations, particularly of leisure tourism activities.

- The climate of beach resort should allow for use of the beach and outdoor recreational facilities for a major portion of the year.
- The beach destination should be conveniently accessible to relatively large number of visitors by air and other modes of transportation. It should be preferably within the radius of maximum of one hour drive from the airport, railway station and important bus terminals.
- It should have proper drinking water supply, electricity, sewerage system, drainage systems and effective communication systems.
- The resort should have general aesthetic features such as attractive topography, flora and founa, regional architectural style, regional life style, local cuisines, shopping and entertainment, sports and recreational facilities, local cultural attractions and if possible entertaining evening hours.
- At last the Committee has emphasised on the need of trained lifeguards.

The recommendations suggested by the Committee, if implemented carefully, are helpful to sustain the environment of any coastal region. Beach tourism is noticed has got prime position in planning and development in the country. But how far we have become successful in adopting the norms and condition laid down not only by the Deptt. of Tourism, Govt. of India but also of Deptt. of Environment have least been considered. It finally decreased satisfaction level and compel to locate some other beach areas for future. In 1991, the Ministry of Environment and Forests (MEF) issued a notification under the Environment (Protection) Act, for regulating the activities in the coastal zone. In the notification, the coastal stretches which are influenced by tidal action (in the land ward side) up to 500 metre from the High Tide Line (HTL), and the land between the Low Tide Line (LTL) and the HTL were declared as Coastal Regulation Zone (CRZ). Within the CRZ, certain activities were prohibited. These include :

- Setting up new industries, and expansion of existing industries, except those directly related to water front or directly needing fore shore facilities;
- Manufacture or handling or storage or disposal of hazardous substances;
- Setting up and expansion of fish processing units including warehousing;
- Setting up and expansion of units/mechanism for disposal of waste and effluents, except facilities required for discharging treated effluents into the water course and for storm water drains;
- Discharge of untreated wastes and effluents from industries, cities or towns and other human settlements.

A Case Study of Goa

Faced with increasing threat to its sensitive ecology and scenic beaches from growing menace of bio-degradable waste, especially plastic littered along the beaches, the Goa government has enacted a law on the lines of Himachal Pradesh to make this a punishable offense. This eco-sensitive touristic state is fast acing major problem of waste, as garbage has been increasing due to large scale bio-medical waste in hospital, rapid urbanisation and expanding tourism industry. The environmental groups here accuse some of the big beach hotels of negligence in disposing their garbage.

According to the legislation passed in the winter session of the State assembly in 1996, anyone found guilty of throwing non-biodegradable garbage especially plastic in public places could face imprisonment for one month and fine of Rs. 5,000. The punishment and fine doubles in case the offender is convicted the second time. The bill also makes it mandatory for owners and occupants of buildings to collect and deposit plastic and other hard waste in public receptacles. The Act seeks to prohibit littering in drains, ventilation shafts, pipe and fittings connected with private and public drainage works any hard waste which would prove a health hazard. On February 13-17, 1995 the United Nations Environment Programme (UNEP) (represented by Helene Genot) and the Economic and Social Commission For Asia and The Pacific (ESCAP) (represented by W. Ponniah) jointly organized a 5-day workshop on Sustainable Coastal Tourism, in Cha-Am, Thailand. The issues raised included sustainable forms of tourism in the coastal areas of Thailand, research-based formulation of guidelines for sustainable coastal tourism development, role of government in the follow-up activities, problems of tourism industry (coastal degradation, missing background information, 'skin-deep' evaluations, socio-cultural concerns and other impacts of tourism caused by the 'bad' tourist). The following needs were identified to making tourism development ecologically and economically viable.

- Transforming guidelines into strategies, tactics and action plans.
- Building partnerships to effectively combat the issues through pragmatic pathways leading to co-operative tourism.
- Re-organizing the priorities for development.
- Community's participation in framing,

implementation and monitoring the development programmes.

- Re-defining the goals for progressive growth.
- Re-structuring political structures to achieve efficiency and commitments.
- Judicious utilisation of EIAs (conducting, complying and enforcing).
- Identification of key persons of right calibre and sincere commitment to influence planning processes.
- Creating awareness and a sense of belonging.
- Involvement of the private sector in bringing about Sustainable Development.

Tej Vir Singh from India, in his paper on 'Coastal Tourism, Conservation and the Community; Case of Goa' made a fervent plea for Cooperative Tourism, community participation and grass root planning for community-based tourism development. Using the example of Goa (India), he explained the occurrance of failure of sustainable tourism development simply because it denied the indigenous hosts of their 'rights' to the empowerment of resources and democracy of development. Referring to the local community as 'folk ecologists' recommended that the over wrought coastlands be returned to them for restoration and preservation.

Other plausible solutions were planning of 'revenue villages', continuous community participation in planning, monitoring and evaluation processes, and most importantly the launching of 'learn to travel campaigns'. He pleaded for the creation of heritage coasts for unique and still undeveloped areas.

5

NGOs ON SUSTAINABLE TOURISM

Sustainable Tourism

Tourism is one of those activities which cuts across different sectors. Several NGOs insist that 'tourism' as an activity is inherently unsustainable as it fosters the use of transport, generates waste in destination areas, consumes water and demands energy, encourages development of new infrastructures, sometimes in the most sensitive locations, and affects the culture of people living in tourist destinations. Moreover, it is stated the high temporal seasonally of tourism with its high peaks in certain seasons leads to high pressures on the receiving areas, resulting in stresses on ecosystems, local culture, transport systems and so on. By and large the NGOs maintain that it is quite doubtful whether something called "sustainable tourism" exists The tourism industry relies on the provision of public goods for its operations. Public goods such as public infrastructure, cultural heritage, landscape, clean air and drinkable water are used as factors of production by the tourism industry. These public goods, which constitute the base of the tourism activity and even the purpose of travelling to other places, can in turn be put under severe pressure by the activity itself. In the case of natural parks and protected areas, this process of self-destruction has been very illustratively described as "loving them to death". Recently, a leading Indian environmentalist stated: "Tourism threatens to become a very major threat to our already traumatised sanctuaries and national parks. Sadly, we must conclude that in addition to dams, mines and other such destructive developmental projects, we must add yet another cause for the decline of wildlife habitats...tourism" Tour operators, the NGOs argue, do not bear the burden of the cost originated by tourism development. They do no face the real costs of the activities they commerce with. As a result, they do not have any incentive to internalise external costs, nor to invest in upgrading public goods. They simply shift towards new destinations when old ones have become unpopular because of overcrowding, degradation of landscape, bad quality of water, both drinking and bathing, and other factors.

Reflection and Action

The UN Conference of Environment and Development held in Rio in 1992 provided the impetus to the tourism industry to engage in a process of reflection and action. The early 90s witnessed thus the creation of environmental branches in businesses, and more importantly a common effort by the tourism industry-both at sectorial level (i.e. hotels, restaurants, tour operators etc.) and as a whole (i.e. the WTTC and its GREEN GLOBE programme)-to take on board (at least at the level of discourse) the concept of sustainable development. At the sectorial level there are a number of organisations which emerged in the early 90s. The most remarkable is the International Hotels Environmental Initiative (IHEI) developed by the global hotel industry for the global hotel industry. The IHEI is led by a Council of 12 of the top hotel companies in the world. Their objective is to promote environmental management as an integral part of running a successful hotel business. Recently, they are thinking of changing their name to something like International Hotels Sustainable Initiative, which very illustratively shows how comfortable industry feels in the sustainable development discourse. Other sectorial initiatives include the Confederation of National Associations of Hotels, Restaurants, Cafes and similar establishments in the European Union and European Economic Area (HOTREC). HOTREC created an Environment Working Group in 1994 whose first task was to elaborate an extensive survey on the environmental initiatives undertaken by its members, namely the 31 national associations located in 18 European countries. At the level of the whole tourism and travel industry the most remarkable initiative is that of the World Travel and Tourism Council (WTTC). WTTC is a global coalition of more than fifty Chief Executive Officers from all sectors of the industry including transportation, accommodation, catering, recreation/cultural and travel services activities. The main goal of the WTTC is to foster the expansion and liberalisation of markets and to eliminate barriers to growth. Against this background, the WTTC created in 1994 GREEN GLOBE, a "worldwide environmental management and awareness programme for the travel and tourism industry". However, GREEN GLOBE actually employs around 5 people in its headquarters in Cambridge (UK). According to Geoffrey Lipman, Chief Executive of GREEN GLOBE and President of the WTTC, GREEN GLOBE is a critical component of their millennium vision goal of sustainable development. There is not one single answer to these questions. Different stakeholders have different perceptions on how this process should be put in place. Existing initiatives to put in place sustainability criteria in industry, trade associations, NGOs and different levels of government, clearly reflect their respective visions.

Nevertheless, there is sometimes some confusion between environmental criteria and sustainability criteria. At this point it is worth mentioning that the environmental dimension is only one of the pillars of sustainable development, and this is equally applicable to the tourist sector. WWF international family feels that it can play an important role in educating industry on a vision of sustainable tourism development which goes beyond the efficient use of resources. However, it would be naive to try to educate industry without having educated ourselves first. Working on sustainable tourism development requires, first and foremost, defining WWF's objectives and programme. There is a need to operationalise the concept of sustainable tourism, fill it in the meaning, and transform it into real policy.

The European Environmental Agency (EEA) is developing a framework to assess the environmental impact of tourism, in particular mass tourism. This framework is based in the elaboration of matrices where different driving forces and environmental impacts are identified. The objective of their work is to assess quantitatively environmental impacts, use of natural resources, water supplies, waste management etc.

Significantly, a major portion of the present tourism business takes place in ecologically sensitive geographical areas and a number of environmentally sensitive regions in the world are also those regions preferred by tourists as their holiday destinations. Tourism cuts across a number of WWF programmes and projects. Very often, sensitive ecosystems can only be protected when the economic activities like tourism lead to impacts on those ecosystems are managed in a way that carrying capacities are not exceeded. Many of WWF programmes and projects are closely related to areas where tourism is a predominant activity or it is likely to become so.

This is the case with coastal areas, marine resources, protected areas, forests and so on. The link between existing projects in the framework of these programmes and the opportunities to take tourism into account in such projects is certainly something to bear in mind when discussing how work at the local level can be articulated. Unfortunately, the major attempts at defining ecotourism and formulating a strategy for sustainable development have remained Eurocentric. The leading international NGOs have met a few times to discuss the issues but invited only the European members. This gave the proceedings a very European perspective. For Asia pacific region, the Male Declaration on Sustainable Development (adopted at the Asia-Pacific Minister's Conference on Tourism and Environment in Maldives on 16 February 1997) has been pathbreaking. This was followed by the draft National Tourism Policy in May 1997 in India. There is an urgent need to have a clearer perspective and an effective strategy. This would require the participation of the industry, the government agencies and the NGOs. And sooner this is done the better.

Admittedly, Tourism is not, a clean and non-polluting industry. A major problem is the lack of a common understanding of what sustainable tourism or "ecotourism" means. This ambiguity leads to violations of environmental regulations and standards. Certainly, the environmental problems evolving from tourism are manifold. First of all, the tourism industry is very resource and land intensive. As such, the interest of the tourism sector will often be in conflict with local resource and land use practices. An influx of tourists into the area will lead to a competition for resources. Employees working at the tourist sites compound this competition. It isevident as a rule, tourists are supplied at the expense of the local population. Remarkably, tourist activities imply an intensified utilisation of vulnerable habitats. Investors and tourists do not necessarily possess awareness on how to use natural resources sustainably, and subsequently this utilisation often leads to a degradation of resources. Tourism is also a major generator of wastes. In most tourist regions of developing countries, sewage, wastewater and solid waste disposal are not properly managed. Finally, tourism is also responsible for a considerable proportion of increased volumes and mileage in global transport and hence the associated environmentally hazardous pollutant emissions. The tourism industry has not shown enough willingness to compensate the cost of conservation of biodiversity in, for instance, protected areas, even though they can profit from it which is a sorrow state of affairs.

Cultural Erosion and Violation of Human Rights

As a proven fact, Tourism is a powerful agent of change. International tourism acts as a catalyst for the transition from traditional ways of life to so-called modern, Western forms of society. Accordingly, tourism often brings with it the introduction of new behaviour trends and norms. Very often, these are contrary to traditional norms existing in the host community, and can come into conflict with its cultural identity and threaten the traditional existing value systems. The problem is that the investors seem to have a lack of cultural understanding of the invested society. There is a need for an increased awareness that establishment of new hotels and resorts. will have its consequences (good or evil) on the society and the people who live in it.

Most often it is noticed that tourism has become associated with violation of human rights. Many destination countries have experienced an increase in criminality, prostitution, alcohol and drug abuse as a consequence of tourism. Furthermore, child labour is commonplace in the tourism industry, more particularly in the informal sector. According to estimates made by ILO, between 3 and 19 million children and teenagers work in the tourism sector. A particularly abominable form of violation of human rights is child slavery and despicable abuse of children taking place in the booming sex industry in many countries. In these countries, tourism has led to an incredible increase in prostitution and also in the exploitation of children. The tourism industry has not yet come up with a general condemnation of these violations of human rights which has become a severe problem which has become a severe problem.

The tourism industry should promote projects, which are compatible with the cultural identity of the local population's way of life. Furthermore, the tourism sector should always make sure it acts in accordance with the cultural heritage, and respect the cultural integrity of tourism destinations. This might be accomplished by defining codes of conduct for the industry and hence providing investors with a checklist for sustainable tourism projects.

Establishing and developing tourist training programmes could be one way of managing codes of conducts for the tourists. Here, tourists can be informed and educated about the destination for their travel both before and after their arrival at the site. At the site, tourist information centres can be established through funding from the investor. The information given to tourists should include codes of conduct regarding appropriate behaviour and clothing. It is reasonable to assume that people's offending behaviour is largely a consequence of ignorance rather than intention. Consequently, information and facts about the destination, ways of life, history, cultural heritage is crucial to help tourists get along.

Absolutely desired, this is a must that tourism investors do not engage in or promote child labour and prostitution. Moreover, it is appropriate that the industry commit themselves to a global campaign against such and any other violation of human rights. Evaluating the sustainability of the tourism development, in regards to cultural and human rights aspects, is highly recommended for those responsible for the tourism projects. As with the case mentioned earlier of preventing environmental degradation, this must be carried out through communication and consultation with the local communities.

Employment and Foreign Exchange Leakage

The tourism industry is characterised by a high degree of monopoly, which implies a concentration of services and profits into very few big transnational corporations. In many countries, tourism facilities mostly belong to foreigners. Furthermore, in local host communities in many countries a relatively small number of people are involved in the tourism industry in host communities in many developing countries. Very often, there is a lack of qualified manpower in the locality. As such, generally most employees are recruited from the big cities, neighbouring countries or even from the country of origin of the investors.

Contrary to popular assumption, Multiplier effects from tourism are less significant. One reason is that tourism industries purchase most of their inputs (materials, products or services) in their country of origin. Rresultantly, a considerable amount of foreign exchange revenues leaks from the destination countries. The more goods, services, physical capital and human capital a country must import for its tourism services, the higher the leakage. Very often the investors are not approaching the local community it actually can provide. Besides this, the General Agreement on Trade in Services (GATS), with its liberalisation of global trade and services, is increasingly undermining the possibilities of individual countries and regions to control their tourism industries and the possible economic gains thereof from.

Local Communities Benefit of Natural Resources

Generally, the tourism industry should engage in promoting sustainability as a hallmark, for investors. More specifically, investors in tourism should strive to adopt environmentally sound technologies or other measures to minimise the consumption of local ground water. In the case of water utilisation, such measures might be water saving equipment, desalination systems and collecting and utilising rainwater. Using other types of resources in a sustainable manner is, of course, also crucial. There is a need to use ecological materials and installation of renewable sources of energy systems (solar energy) in all new buildings and new construction. Again, there should be an acceleration of installation or solar/wind power in all public work projects of communities where tourism will be introduced. To prevent or minimise the impact of chemical inputs in soil, water and health, one should start utilising sound ecological methods, including Integrated Pest Management. Ecological methods need to be applied in all areas utilised for tourism, including in the maintenance of golf courts, gardens and recreational facilities etc.

Strictly, Pollution of ground and coastal waters must be prevented, and recommendations must be made (perhaps even legislation) for tourism investors to 'invest in proper sewage treatment facilities. Appropriate waste disposal systems and ways to separate garbage into organic and non-organic waste should be developed. Organic waste can be composted and possibly reused on hotel gardens or even for local farming. This could be done through collaboration with local residents. Residents could organise themselves and manage the allocated dumping sites, and hence benefit from the system in receiving payment from the hotel for services rendered. A system to separate the different materials, and recycle some should be in place at the landfill site, thus further reducing the waste.

To avoid degradation of the natural environment, tourism projects can help finance protected areas and safeguard ecologically sensitive regions against further environmental deterioration. By empowering local populations and have them participating in the entire process, sustainability will be ensured as it become: accepted by and adjusted to the local communities. Also, a protected area might certainly be a suitable tourist-attraction, where tourists can experience amazing nature and learn about conservation and traditional uses of natural resources in the area.

As a social obligation, investors in tourism should always respect the traditional land tenure system in the area and the traditional user.-right systems of resources. In this connection, the communication and consultation with the local communities about resource-use is important. Tourism investors should not exclude local people from using local resources, and thus take away what they depend on for survival in fitness. The tourism industry can and must take initiatives to implement that polluter(s) pay a principle (or other forms of internalisation of externalities) for pollution related to tourism operations. This may be organised and carried out through local tax systems or through funds established by the tourism industry for local community development. However, the paid principle should be applied for minor pollution only and should not be developed into a possibility for investors to pay a symbolic fine for imposed irreversible negative impacts on the local environment. Inaccurate and/or mild environmental legislation in destination countries may possibly attract more foreign investors contributing to fast economic growth and development, but with environmental damage as a consequence.

To avoid the dilemma, destination countries will have to choose between economic development and environmental protection. Multinational enterprises must be committed to follow the environmental standards of their home country should these be stricter than those at the destinations, which is the need of hour.

By devising local training programmes and establishing educational projects, the tourism industry can ensure that qualified local people are employed in their projects. One should train the local people instead of foreigners to become guides due to their knowledge of the area and resources. The investors should be responsive to the kind of knowledge, abilities and skills found in the local communities. Very often such knowledge and skills are well fitted to be used-in tourist activities be it fishing trips, nature trails, souvenir sales or dancing courses for tourists etc.

For checking foreign exchange leakage, those responsible for the tourism projects should ensure that local inputs are purchased for their projects. A proper examination of local resources available will be beneficial for both the industry and the local residents. Usually, there is considerable local willingness to start producing new products if a market for these products exists. The tourism sector should also adopt measures to prevent foreign exchange leakage by a commitment to re-investment of a fair share of the locally accrued profit. Mention is already made of protected areas, training programmes on codes of conduct for tourists, or possible training of local employees, as projects in need of funds: Initiatives towards more local community development projects should also be appropriate for ameliorating the situation.

As an affirmative action, the tourism industry should promote the establishment of small and medium-sized tourism enterprises which, compared to large-scale hotels etc., have far more moderate impacts on the environment. It is the industry's responsibility to act as a model for communities to show that it is possible to do business whilst protecting natural resources. The industry should also promote and support local communities to start tourism-related businesses and grant access to low interest loans. It is the responsibility of the tourism sector to ensure total transparency in all transactions, and to prevent tourism projects from being used as projects for laundering illicit money, as well as to refuse using bribes as a means to obfuscate or avoid government rules and regulations. There should be a global boycott against those investors involved in such or other types of illegal activities.

Suggestions and Recommendations

Empowerment of residents at tourist destinations, through local participation, may be facilitated by providing written and legally binding contracts between local people and tourism investors/developers. The contracts will help avoid broken promises, which too many examples and previous experience prove to be a big problem. Besides the mentioned examples of providing proper information for tourists and establishing training programmes for residents, the tourism industry, through for instance the WTTC or the WTO with NGOs in the selection panels, could issue awards especially for sustainable tourism projects as an encouragement for investors which may have positive impact and results.

Within the tourism and hospitality industry, it is important that both small and large-scale tourism operators are included in the collaboration and that they participate in solving problems related to tourism development. Obviously a sustainable development of the tourism industry can only be ensured through participation of all local residents in the destination countries. There is a need for a willingness and ability for the partners to work with this kind of bottom-up approach. In this context, both environment and social NGOs have an important role to play, putting pressure on the industry and facilitating contracts and local participation for community development. Governments in both destination and countries of origin of tourists and investors are responsible for providing appropriate legislation for sustainable tourism development, and to follow up the tourism projects with sufficient monitoring and appropriate sanctioning. Exchange of successful experiences of sustainable tourism projects is an important factor in this connection. Finally, an interdisciplinary approach to the problem is necessary: using local, regional and/or international consultative forums.

Taking note of the above will lead the entire industry and community at destination towards sustainable development as well as sustainable tourism.

Tour Operators Initiative for Sustainable Tourism Development

As the largest industry in the world, tourism makes a significant positive contribution to economic development The industry also makes major demands on natural resources and creates significant environmental and social impacts, often in places where resources are vulnerable or scarce. To maintain the attraction of existing destinations, and develop new ones, the tourism industry needs to work closely with other stakeholders to devise and implement strategies for sustainable development. The aim is to meet the needs of people today without jeopardising the ability of future generations to meet their own needs.

Meeting the Needs or Today

There is no doubt environmental and social issues will have an increasingly significant effect on the way the tourism industry conducts itself. The future of the tourism business demands the development of new tools and practices to encourage the improvement of environmental performance while at the same time meeting commercial needs.

Tour Operators Initiative

The Tour Operators' Initiative is aimed at improving the sustainability of the tourism industry. Developed by tour operators for Tour Operators', this voluntary Initiative is supported by major international organisations including the United Nations Environment Programme (UNEP), United Nations Educational Scientific and Cultural Organisation (UNESCO) and the World Tourism Organisation. The Tour Operators' Initiative facilitates a partnership network between interested Tour Operators' of all sizes and acts as a platform to develop ideas and projects and to share and learn from the experiences of members.

Meeting the Needs of the Business

Sustainability is no threat to tourism, the very opposite in fact A tourism product which cannot be sustained, deteriorates or becomes damaged, will instantly pay the same price as any uncompetitive commodity. Its customers will abandon it for a rival that provides better value. To ensure the profitable future of tourism we have to work towards sustainability and maintain the quality of the raw material of tourism. The benefits will be:

- Risk management in future destination development
- A better variety and quality of tourism product
- Appeal to an increasingly discriminating public
- Cost saving through energy and waste management
- Build links with communities and cultures affected by tourism
- Benefit from the backing of UNEP, UNESCO and WTO
- Association with an ethically and environmentally responsible approach to tourism
- Improved company image internally and externally.

Our Commitment

Founding members of the Initiative have committed to developing sustainable tourism using a collective voice to influence the actions of governments, developers, tourist boards, customers and suppliers. Tour Operators' signing the Initiative are asked to join us in our commitment to:

- introduce environmental policy and management systems into their operations
- monitor and report our progress implementing sustainable tourism practices
- promote sustainable tourism to suppliers, contractors and customers.

A range of activities and resources to help create a better business with lower environmental and social impacts will be available:

- workshops and conferences
- national and regional working groups on key environmental and sustainability issues
- education and training
- publications and information-including a newsletter, best practice archive and the Tour Operators' Initiative website.

Good Practices in Sustainable Tourism

Members of the Tour Operators' Initiative are adopting hood practices that include:

Working with accommodation suppliers: Inclusion of environmental clauses in contracts, and provision of environmental management guidance manuals and checklists.

Improving transport's environmental profile: Use of rail travel in preference to air and road transport.

6

NATURAL TOURISM RESOURCES OF INDIA

> "Leonardo da Vinci was in habit of paying the price demanded by the owners of captive birds for pleasure of setting them free."

As a prescribed standard, there should be least 33 per cent area of forest in a country. For ecological balance there should be 60 per cent forests on the hilly mountainous terrain and 20 per cent forest cover on plains. Dismally, in India, the data shows we have 22.8 per cent area under forest, but the recent satellite pictures show that we have hardly 10 per cent to 11 per cent forest area. These forests are natural habitat for the wild animals. So the number and variety of wild life is affected by the expansion and shrinking of natural habitat. India, being the 7th largest country, is the country where all representative animals are found. There is no single species, which is found in neighbourhood, but not in India. There are transition zones, e.g., the fauna of Indian Thar desert is also common in Pakistan. The animals of dry Himalayas (Ladakh) are common in India and Nepal. Other Himalaya and Terai animals are common in India, Nepal, and Bhutan. The wild animals of Ganga-Brahmaputra plain and delta are common in India as well as Bangladesh. Similar is the case with peninsular India and Sri Lanka. Indian subcontinent has very important place on the wild life map of the world. There are about five hundred species of mammals, more than two thousand species of birds, many species of fish, reptiles, amphibians and more than 30,000 forms of insects found in this subcontinent. The Asiatic lion, the armoured one horned great Indian rhinoceros, the magnificent Royal Bengal tiger, the massive Indian elephant and the large Indian gaur are the big five of our forests. They are comparable only with their counterpart animals of Africa where heavy Ethiopian lion, big eared Elephant, two homed rhinoceros, etc. are found. India is the only country in the world where lion and, tiger both are found. The three species of cats including the spotted, marbled, fishing, desert, golden, jungle, pallas, the caracal types of cats and the lynx are found. The white tiger is very unique to India. India has twelve species of bats including the flying fox or fruit bat, the flying lemur, which is neither a lemur nor bat, but bears the same relationship to the shrews as the flying squirrel does to tile squirrels. There are four species of apes in the, world, among them mighty gorilla are intelligent. Chimpanzees are found in Africa, orangutan, and gibbon are found in Asia; India has the noisiest ape—the hoolock. There are 5 species of monkeys- the rhesus, the bonnest, the lion tailed, the Assamese and the pigtailed. There are two species of lemurs-the slow Loris and the slender Loris found in Sikkim and Bhutan. The long tailed monkeys—Human, the golden langur, the capped and nilgiri langur are peculiar features of peninsula. Hares and Rabbits are widely distributed in subcontinent. They are found from desert to snow capped hills and from open to thick forests to thinly forested areas. Rabbits are born naked while hares are covered with hair. There are about 1729 species of rodents in the world; they are also widely distributed in South Asian countries. They are squirrels, antelopes rats, rats etc. Water in Ganga river has not flown much when the wild animals were widely distributed in Indian subcontinent.

Remarkably upto Mughal period wild flora as well as fauna was abundant. But after the arrival of Britishers, due to expansion of their various economic and commercial activities like mining, plantation, roads-railways construction, etc. and later in on the world wars, a large sum of forests were swept away and the wild animals were killed in very massive amount. In this century many species, which were abundant, came in the verge of extinction. So the need of leaving some law to protect them was felt. It was also thought that there would be some areas where the animals can refuge themselves in their natural environment. So the concepts of many categories of forests developed such as National Parks, Sanctuary, protected area, reserves etc.

The Indian Board of Wildlife, which is mainly responsible for the management, preservation and development of wild fauna and flora, has defined four areas where wild life receives some kind of protection. Under the provision of Wildlife (Protection) Act, 1972, any area can be declared by the State government as a sanctuary or national park in case the concerned area needs protection and conservation for its ecological, faunal, floral, geomorphological and zoological significance. The Central government can establish a sanctuary or national park with the consent of the concerned State governments of India.

NATIONAL PARKS

According to the Indian Board for Wildlife, "a National Park is an area dedicated by statute the scenery, natural and historical objects, to conserve the wildlife there in and to provide for enjoyment of the same in such manner and by such means, that will leave them unimpaired for the enjoyment of future generations with such modification as local conditions may demand. In the most countries of the world, the national, central or federal government of the country can only create a National Park. But in India a State government can constitute a National Park in its State Legislature-preferably subject to certain standards, which are now being drawn by the Indian Board of wildlife. The history of National parks in India begins in 1936 when the Hailey (now Corbett) National Park Uttarkhand, was created. The definition of national parks evolved in 1933 at the London Conference of African Fauna, according to which a national park is an area placed under public control, the boundaries of which shall not be altered except by competent legislative authority. The area is declared for the protection and preservation for all time of wild animals life and wild vegetation for the benefit and advantage and enjoyment of the general public. In this area hunting of fauna or collection of flora is prohibited except under the direction of park authority.

Sanctuary

The Indian Board for Wildlife has defined a sanctuary as,' An "area where killing, hunting, shooting or capturing of any species of bird or animals is prohibited except by or under the control of highest authority in the department responsible for the management of the sanctuary and whose boundaries and character should be sacrosanct as far as possible'. The Board has further clarified the position by stating that while the management of sanctuaries does not involve suspension or restriction of normal forest operation, it is desirable to aside a completely sacrosanct area within a sanctuary to be known as 'Abhyaranya'. It has also indicated that sanctuaries should' be made accessible to the public. In India sanctuary in usually created by an order or gazette notification of State government. So the weakness of a sanctuary is that it can be desanctuarised merely by another order or gazette notification of a State government because it is not safeguarded by any proper legislation. The idea behind a wild life sanctuary and a national park is same, i.e., maximum protection, preservation and conservation of wild animals. But the fundamental difference between the two is that a sanctuary is created by order of a competent authority, who any be the Chief Conservator of forests or minister of a State, while a national park can be formed, abolished or changed only by the legislation of a State.. Therefore, the status and degree of permanency and protection is much higher in a national park than in a sanctuary. In a wild life sanctuary private ownership rights may continue and forestry and other usages also may continue so long as wild life conservation is not adversely affected.

However, in a national park all private ownership rights are extinguished and all forestry and other usages are prohibited. Every national park should have the minimum requisites of fauna, flora and scenery etc. There should be sufficient means of management and protection in a sanctuary to be upgraded as national park. Before declaring any forest as a national park, it must be confirmed that the area is of sufficient importance and status to deserve the appellation. Administration of such area must be improved and illegalities such as poaching and unauthorised gazing should be eliminated. The size of the park must be adequate, the boundaries should be well chosen and buffer zones should be provided against shooting, grazing and cultivation. Both sanctuaries and national parks may be formed out of reserved or protected forests and wherever forest products extraction is unavoidable, there must be an inner sanctuary or Abhyaranya, where no disturbances should be allowed. Central government provides assistance to the State governments for sanctuaries as well as for national parks.

Protected Area

The Indian Board for wild life describes a protected area, In many States there may be are as where it may be considered expedient, (i) to afford special protection to wild life, in order to enable species of wildlife which are on the verge of extinction to reestablish themselves, (ii) to afford protection to wild life attracted to water impounded in river valley projects and to other irrigation works, (iii) to afford protection to wild life in and around large towns and sacred place. Such areas may be constituted as protected area by an order of the government who may also fix the degree of protection and period of protection (may be temporary or permanent). Elaborating this definition Gee has clarified that protection of wild life does not necessarily imply the protection of vermin. Those wild animals and birds etc. which are injurious to other animals, or to the man in short or long term, can be kept under the control or even destroyed altogether in extreme case in certain places. In November 1972 the Indian Wild Life Board chose the tiger as the national animal of India. A national scheme called the 'Project Tiger' was launched to protect the tiger population. At present there are 16 tiger reserves in India, of these 4 are wild life sanctuaries and 12 are national parks. In India there were 63 national parks and 363 wild life sanctuaries in 1987. Indian subcontinents has grown with British legacy.

Legislation, Development and Impact of Wildlife

After independence Government of India made some plans for the development of forests and their natural habitats. National forest policy was the first step in this direction in which one third of geographic area was aimed to achieve as forest areas (60 per cent in plains and 20 per cent in hill areas) for ecological balance and preservation of wild life. Government of India is conscious for the preservation and development of wild life and has taken many steps in the direction. Among these steps the most important is the financial assistance to States for the development of sanctuaries and national parks.

Plan Allocation for Wild Life Sanctuaries

There is a total outlay of Rs. 360 lakh for the seventh plan period under the centrally sponsored schemes 'Assistance to States for development of sanctuaries' Financial assistance is given to the States after scrutiny of their proposals on 100 per cent basis for items on non-recurring expenditure and on the condition that the wild life sanctuary being financed is under the complete control of that State's wild life wing. The budget provision for the development of 105 sanctuaries in 1987-88 was Rs 200 lakhs, which increased up to Rs. 275 lakhs for the year 1988-89 and further to Rs. 625 lakhs in 2000-01.

Plan Allocation for National Park

During sixth plan there was an allocation of only Rs. 99 lakh for the development of national parks, which was raised to Rs. 260 lakhs in Seventh plan period. Under the central scheme of' assistance to States for development of national parks' given to States after scrutiny of their proposal, on 100 per cent basis for items of recurring expenditure and on 50 per cent basis for items of recurring expenditure. The conditions that the national park being financed is under the complete control of the State's wild life wing. The budget provision for the development of 32 national parks in 1987-88 was Rs: 199 lakh and during 1988-89 it is Rs. 192 lakh. In November 1972 the Indian Wildlife Board chose the tiger as the national animal of India. A national scheme called the 'Project Tiger' was launched to protect the dangerously depleting species. There are "16 tiger projects in India of which four are wild life sanctuaries and 12 are national parks. These tiger reserves get special attention and allocated from center. In present plan Namdapha, Palamu, Nagarjun Sagar etc. are important reserves that have got special attention. The Directorate of Wildlife under the Ministry of Environment and Forest was set up in pursuance of guidelines were given by the National Wild life Action Plan to assist the State government in the proper management of the national parks and sanctuaries. The Directorate is also responsible for assigning the assistance to States. Its efforts to enlarge the network of wildlife-protected areas to adequately represent country's biological diversity were continued during 1988. By the end of 1988 there were 68 national parks and 366 sanctuaries in the country. The Wild Life institute of India has completed a project for preparation of the biogeographic classification suitable for conservation; planning and has submitted a report entitled 'Planning a Wildlife Protected Area Network in India'. The report recommended that at least 4.6 per cent of geographic area of the country should be under national parks/ sanctuaries. At present it is 4.07 per cent. The Indian Board for Wildlife, the apex statutory advisory body for formulating policies on wild life, the management of various national parks had been evaluated by a committee appointed by the Board and Dachigham national park was adjudged the best national park for the year 1981-'84. The Indian Board for Wild life has played an important role in encouraging and growing consciousness among the people for wild life. It organises various programmes, functions, seminars and workshops for conservation of wild life during wild life week, which is celebrated in first week of October. The British were responsible for the large-scale deforestation and mass destruction of the wild life. But they were also the people who became aware of their preservation and tried to regulate various laws. During that period British administrators passed various acts. The Indian Forest Act (1879,1927,1950) and its adaptations in States was administered by the forest departments and gave basic protection to wild life in reserved and protected forests as follows:

- Prohibition of shooting, fishing and poisoning water, setting of traps and snares; Section 26(i) Reserved forests, Section 32(j) Protected forests.
- Prohibition of killing or capturing of elephants in areas where the Elephant Preservation Act of 1879 is not in force. Section 26(j) Reserved forests. Section 33 (j) Protected forests.

Indian addition to the Indian Forest Act, there was the 1887 act for the preservation of wild bird and game, or the "Wild Birds and Animals Protection Act" as it became in 1912. This act was applicable to all types of areas and in areas outside the reserves, which was administered by the civil and police departments of the States to which it has been extended, though in reality it was a dead letter. The act was applied to few specified wild birds and animals from time to time. Close reasons were declared for them.

At that the penalties were fine up to Rs. 50 and for every subsequent conviction, imprisonment up to one month or fine up to Rs. 100 or both. Besides these acts, certain legislations applicable to certain places and time were also in existence, such as the Elephant Preservation Act of 1879, the Indian Fisheries Act 1897, the Assam Rhinoceros Preservation Act and the Bengal Rhinoceros Protection Act. After Independence the Bombay State (Maharashtra) Wild Birds and Animals Protection Act of 1951 was first step and was 'also recommended as a model for other States. This Act brought all types of areas; whether government forests or waste lands under the same law and the same set of rules, and this undoubtedly makes for simplicity of administration and control. The conservator of forests was empowered as special wild life preservation officer, assisted by Game wardens (Divisional forest officers or Deputy collectors). The main machinery of enforcement is the forest department itself or revenue patel in the absence of forest staff. All forms of shooting and trapping of wild life were licenced. Penalty and imprisonment for offence was also fixed. Many other States also modified their acts in more or less same line. Wildlife (Protection) Act 1972 is the recent and most scientific protection measures taken to preserve the vanishing species. Under the provision of this act, any area can be declared as a wild life sanctuary or a national park in case the area concerned needs protection and conservation for its ecological, faunal, floral, geomorphological and zoological significance. The Central government can establish a wild life sanctuary or national park with the consent of the concerned State government. Efforts to control poaching and illegal trade in wild life by strict implementation of this act were stepped up through the four regional offices. Financial assistance to twelve States to the tune of Rs. 30 lakh is being provided to tackle the problem of illegal killing of wild animals, particularly elephant in the southern States and has had a marked impact. To gather timely and correct intelligence about poachers and illegal traders, a system of cash awards both under the central sector and centrally sponsored schemes was introduced. In the cases of offences relating to species included in Schedule I and Schedule II, Part II of the act, or to hunting in national park or sanctuary, the offender shall be liable for punishment for a term which shall not be less than six months, can be extended to six years and also with fine which shall not be less than five hundred rupees. In case of a subsequent offence the term of imprisonment shall not be less than one year and the fine shall not be less than one thousand rupees. The causes are compoundable. Officers not below the rank of Deputy Conservator of forests are empowered to accept a sum up to Rs. 2000/ by way of compensation of such offences. In this act it is also mentioned that the wild animals, meat trophy, incurred trophy, animal article, in respect to which an offence has been committed under this act shall be property of the government.

Impact of Tourism Wildlife

Till 1970s no serious attempt was made to exploit tourism potentialities in national parks and sanctuaries. But the enactment of Wildlife (protection) Act, 1972 was significant step in the encouragement of tourism. Before this law wild life tourism was disorganised and haphazard. The tourists were not enthusiastic to visit the forest knowing that poachers and other elements might have wiped out or driven away the wild animals. After enforcement of the new measures, the strict restriction on hunting and building of infrastructures through financial aid by central government the tourism began to develop. They were not only encouraged for seeing wild animals, but natural flora also. Wild life tourism has made people more conscious of nature conservation. Though it has also been alleged that tourism has led to the degradation of fauna of sanctuaries and parks: But guided wild life tourism can never lead to degradation of wild Life sanctuaries and parks. However, the wild life tourism could not grow substantially in India. Only in the case of Sariska and Periyer a marginal growth is recorded. Our wild life tourism constitutes hardly 5 to 10 per cent foreign tourists. There many reasons behind this state lack of infrastructure like all season roads- hotel accommodations, vehicles and lack of properly trained guides.

Public consciousness and enthusiasm about wild life and nature has not grown so much, which can boost wild life tourism. Other parks and sanctuaries, which are far from important places, have yet to do a lot for development. So, the, impact of tourism on tribal community is also not countrywide but limited to few places. The decade of 1975 was most favourable for wild animals when these silent creatures were protected under the umbrella or various laws and acts plans and projects. In 1970 tiger hunting was banned when Kailash Sankla a forest officer and former Director of Project Tiger, drew attention to the plight of tigers in International Union for Conservation of Nature and Natural Resources Congress (New Delhi 1969). Tiger was included in Red data book. The result was the setting up the Project Tiger. The next important step was the Wildlife (Protection) Act of 1972. Thereafter the state-central government tried to pay proper attention on the preservation of wild life. Due to such efforts many species revised for example tiger, black buck crocodile various types of monkeys etc. Though many cases of offences have also been reported were wild creatures were hunted by poachers for instance since '1982 four tiger and many dozens black bucks were killed in Sariska alone. There is other face of wild life problem too. A new problem has emerged new, that is the increasing/increased numbers of many species of animals have created problems to the people living in nearby villages. This problem was highlighted in the Conference of State forest minister (May '89, New Delhi). S.N. Medhi, the forest minister of Assam was too annoyed because the elephants have killed hundreds of people. They raid the crops and killed people if they come in the way. At present Assam has largest elephant population around 5,000 elephants in 5,000 sq. km. Crocodiles create other headache. In 1975 project crocodiles was launched to save this reptile from extinction. The project was successful and they grew three times. One third of them were released into rivers, but there are still above 7,000 in 32 farms of the country. The fisherman of those areas where these crocodiles attacked them and absorbed the fish population. In desperation many States proposed that they would sell crocodile skins in lucrative prices abroad. Initially the Environment Ministry agreed for it and even set up a Pilot Project for 'farming Crocodiles' in Tamil Nadu, but the ecologists opposed it and the government was compelled to stop this project. Similar was the case with other well-known projects. The Project Tiger succeeded in increasing the population reported that more than 450 people have been killed by tigers since 1978 in Dudhwa (U.P.). Cattle lifting is a common phenomena. The people of Sunder ban, Ranthambhor and other reserves are always afraid of these animal terrorists. The Lions, though not much in number are also wandering out of reserve area. The most unfortunate situation is that the people who traditionally protected these animals are turning against them. The Bishnoi community around Jodhpur has protected black population for centuries. Now they are in large numbers (around

12,000) and damage their crops. Similar is the case of nilgai of Rajasthan who became abundant and always raided the crops of villagers. Such incidents have caused the people around sanctuaries and parks to be 'anti-conservationists'. For instance, in Dudhwa, villagers who were fed up with their cattle being lifted regularly poisoned five tigers. Similar case of poisoning the lion in Gir has also come into light, The Director of the Project Tiger Dr. R.L. Singh has admitted that around 40,50 people became victims of tigers annually. The local people are raising their voices against this project because they are threatened with tigers and feel that land is encroached by tiger reserves where they are deprived of fodder. Such dilemma has triggered of a nation wide debate about what to do with excessive numbers. Some are advocating for hunting also. But Dr. Ranjit Singh (Additional Secretary Ministry of Environment and Wildlife) a well known conservationist disagrees on this idea because if once their killing is allowed it would be very difficult to regulate it. It would lead to misuse and destruction of wildlife. Mr. H.S. Pawar, Director Wildlife Institute of India, Dehradun, has rightly pointed out that local abundance of a species does not mean that it is out of danger. It means that it present habitat is insufficient. Real problem does not lie in the protection and conservation but in the management and planning of reserves. The original Project Tiger plan envisaged buffer zones around protected core, meant to take care of any pillover of tigers while allowing people from adjoining villages to forage. But so far the project officials have totally failed in preserving the buffer zones. The reality is that most of India's wild animals are pushed into 363 plus 63 sanctuaries and parks, which account for barely 4 per cent of country's geographical area. These forest areas have also been encroached by villagers. Traditional corridors, which enabled the animals to move from one forest to next, have been cut off. The Gir lions are living in an isolated small patch. They can be wiped out by just one epidemic. Even the protected parks and sanctuaries are not free from human intrusion and cattle grazing. A study done by Indian Institute of Public Administration found that about 50 per cent of parks and 70 per cent of the sanctuaries, the people are living inside the core zones. Most of buffer zones have disappeared and the fringes of these sanctuaries have turned into major battleground between man and animals. Now the Ministry of Environment has taken vital steps of identifying corridors between forests to enable movements of animals. The Wildlife Institute of India Dehradun has already submitted a blue print for developing corridors in all geographic regions in the country which will provide an additional 42 thousand sq km protected area to animals. But it seems a difficult task to acquire land from villagers from these corridors and rehabilitating them elsewhere. The ecologists are also concentrating on the development of buffer zones. In the buffer zones areas for human use would be clearly demarcated. Here with the help of villagers in surroundings areas fuel and fodder would be grown to meet their needs and the remaining parts would be developed for animals to roam around freely. All these plans raise optimism and one can expect in next coming years Homo sapiens the wisest creature, will learn to live with these silent creatures. He will not only think about himself but about the irreplaceable nature and nature's inhabitants.

A Dilemma

Sanctuaries and National Parks have been created for exclusively protecting the wild flora and fauna in all parts of the world and in India, as a part of broad wild-life management prospective. These are the last resort of wildlife and as such prevent it from disappearance. Under the Wildlife (Protection) Act, 1972, the State Governments are empowered to declare any area as a Sanctuary or a National Park as per the procedure laid down, for the purpose of protecting, propagating or developing wildlife or its environment. At present, in India there are 85 National parks comprising an area of about 6471.22 sq km and 448 sanctuaries spread over an area of 69,292 sq km. The total area under Sanctuaries and National Parks comprises 19% of the reserved forest area of the country and 2.3 per cent of the total geographical area. An expert committee has recommended that about 4% of the total geographical area should be brought under National Parks and Sanctuaries. Even before the independence sanctuaries have been created in the form of shooting blocks, game reserves or hunting reserves by the Provincial Governments or by the native rulers in their respective areas. In 1936 the first National Park in India was created and named as the Hailey National Park, in Uttaranchal (formerly Uttar Pradesh), now known, as Corbett National Park. Sanctuaries, National Parks, Game reserves and closed areas are dealt of the Wildlife (Protection) Act, 1972 (53 of 1972) from sections 18 to 38. Sections 18 to 34 deal with Sanctuaries, section 35 with National Parks and sections 36 and 37 with Game reserves and closed areas respectively. Section 38 empowers the Central Government to declare areas as Sanctuaries and National Parks. The Central Government control over Forest and Wildlife has further increased through the 42nd Constitutional amendment bin when those subjects were transferred to concurrent list. The enactment of Forest Conservation Act 1980 has further increased the power of Central Government over Forestlands.

Sanctuaries. Under section 18 "The State Government

may, by notification dec/are any area to be a Sanctuary if it considers that such area is of adequate *ecological*, fauna/, *floral*, geomorphological natural or *zoological significance, for the purpose of Protecting, propagating or developing wild life or its environment*" When any area has been declared as Sanctuary the Collector shall enquire into and determine the existence, 'nature and extent of the rights of any persons in or over the land comprised within the limit of Sanctuary. And after the enquiry, settlement of right and acquisition of the land as per provision of the act, no person is allowed to move freely inside the Sanctuary area except on the permission of the Sanctuary authorities. The permanent residents of the area are also bound to perform certain duties such as helping the authorities to prevent the commission of any offence, to help in controlling fire damage, to report about the dead wild animals, and to render all kinds of help in arresting the offenders. The Chief Wildlife Warden may authorise any person to enter or reside inside the Sanctuary for the purpose of investigation or study of wild-life and purpose ancillary or incidental thereto photography, scientific, research, tourism or transaction of lawful business with any person residing in the Sanctuary on payment of prescribed fee. The permission granted can, however, be cancelled by the Chief Wildlife Warden or Wildlife Warden or any other Sanctuary authority, authorised for the purpose. Inside a Sanctuary the carrying of weapon with out permission, setting fire to Sanctuary or candle any fire or leave any fire burning, use of explosives and chemicals are strictly prohibited. For the purpose of efficient management of the Sanctuary, Chief Wild Life Warden or any other officer empowered on his behalf can take all such steps which he thinks proper, for the security of wild animals in the Sanctuary and may regulate, control or prohibit, in keeping with the interest of wild-fife, the grazing or fishing or movement of cattle. Any person residing within the 10 km of such sanctuary and possessing license of arms shall have to register his name in the office of Chief Wild Life Warden.

National Parks. Under section 35 "whenever it appear to the State Government that an area, whether within a sanctuary or not is by reason or its ecological, faunal, floral, geomorphological or zoological association or importance, needed to be constituted as a National Park for the purpose of propagating or developing wild-life therein or its environment it may, by notification, declare its intention to constitute such area as a National Park". The last few words of the definition differentiate between the Sanctuary and the National Park. Whereas the Sanctuary-should be of natural or zoological significance, a National Park should be of zoological association or importance. After notification of the intention of the State Government for declaring an area to be a National Park, due enquiry will be made and after settling the rights and acquisition of the land by the collector, the area shall be declared as a National Park by the State Government by another notification giving details of the limits of the area. No alteration of the boundaries of a National Park shall be made except on a resolution passed by the Legislature of the State. All kinds of destruction, exploitation and removal of Wildlife and any damage in the habitat of any animal is strictly prohibited inside a National Park.

However, the Chief Wildlife Warden may issue permit after prior approval of the State Government, if such destruction, exploitation and removal of wildlife and its habitat is essential for the better management and improvement in the overall conditions of wild-life in the National Park. Under no circumstances grazing of cattle is permitted inside the National Park. Under section 36, the State Government by notification may declare any area to be a game reserve and no hunting of any wild animal is permitted in such a reserve except with prior permission of the Chief Wild Life Warden or the authorised Officer. Further under section 27, the State Government by notification may declare any area closed to hunting for the period as mentioned in the notification.

National Certification Systems for Sustainable Tourism: WTO Recommendations

Certification systems for sustainable tourism play an increasing role in regulating tourism operations as voluntary instruments above legal frameworks. They usually address three main aspects, namely: 1) environmental performance of companies, operations and destinations; 2) product quality; and 3) corporate social responsibility of operations. They normally target tourism suppliers, such as accommodation, restaurants, sport and leisure facilities, tourist attractions, destinations, tour operators, (tourist) transport companies, tourist associations, etc.

Considering the growing number and importance of certification systems and other voluntary initiatives in tourism, and based on a recommendation made by the UN Commission on Sustainable Development, WTO undertook a comprehensive worldwide study on this topic. The results of this study were published in 2002, under the title "Voluntary Initiatives for Sustainable Tourism: Worldwide Inventory and Comparative Analysis of 104 Eco-labels, Awards And Self-commitments".

The WTO Committee on Sustainable Development of Tourism, at its 3rd Session held in Costa Rica, 25-26 September 2002 recommended the preparation of a set of guidelines for Governments on certification systems for sustainable tourism. Acting on this decision of the Committee, the present document aims at enhancing awareness among governments about the opportunities certification systems may provide as part of their sustainable development policy goals, and provides basic recommendations for supporting and/or establishing such systems at the national level. It is primarily based on the WTO study mentioned above. It also draws on the survey conducted among WTO Member States in November 2001 - January 2002, considering the feasibility of a Sustainable Tourism Stewardship Council, on the experience gained in the area of certification through the International Year of Ecotourism 2002, on comments received from the Committee members, and on other relevant documents.

The Role of Governments in Present Certification Systems

The WTO study on voluntary initiatives for sustainable tourism revealed that governments have an important role in many of the certification systems presently operating. Twenty of the 59 certification schemes investigated are lead by government agencies. A further 18 have government involvement, either through direct financial support, marketing support, expert know-how in criteria setting, verification procedures, or surveillance of procedures followed by the certification body. Government financial support is crucial to half the schemes for which data is available. Government agencies involved generally include either environment ministries, national tourism authorities and tourist boards, and in fewer cases, standards institutes.

Certification systems can bring benefits to society, the environment, governments, private companies and consumers as well.

Potential benefits for society:

- Generally speaking, societies will benefit from certification systems that cover the three aspects of sustainability: social, environmental and economic. Certified companies are supposed to generate benefits in these three areas, while reducing their negative impacts. Therefore, the contribution of tourism activities to the sustainable development of host societies will be more evident, more measurable and more accountable.
- Furthermore, the level of awareness on sustainability issues will be stronger in the host society if the large majority of tourism companies and/or destinations are certified.

Potential benefits for the environment:

- It is evident that certification systems and ecolabels that include strict environmental criteria result in benefits for the local environment and, to the extent that some mass tourism activities can impact biodiversity and climate change, also the global environment.
- Furthermore, the widespread use of ecolabels and certification systems in the tourism industry helps to generate increased environmental awareness among both, tourists and host societies and should result in more caring attitudes with respect to the natural and built environments.

Potential benefits for governments:

- Providing an effective alternative to direct

regulation, which could prove more difficult and time-consuming to implement;

- Enabling governments to adopt a flexible approach to monitoring the tourism industry, permitting organisations to proceed at the pace they feel most comfortable with, while encouraging them to develop innovative approaches to environmental and socio-cultural improvements;
- Giving tourism companies greater scope for making environmental and social improvements by exploiting opportunities specific to their individual circumstances, rather than governments having to control and inspect companies in order to check that they comply with general, industry-wide regulations;
- Allowing part of the costs of implementing and monitoring environmental protection measures to be transferred to the industry itself, thereby reducing the financial burden of regulation on the taxpayer;
- National programs of tourism certification can enhance tourism's recognition in the country, national competitiveness and image in international markets.

Potential benefits for companies:

- Adherence to voluntary environmental initiatives can enable the company to market its products more effectively, and to improve their public image among consumers, business partners and with the host communities;
- Engaging in voluntary certification can help

companies to signal their specific commitment to environmental, social and even economic improvements, which may in turn help to defer the need for further direct regulation by governments;

- Pursuing sound environmental management strategies can generate substantial cost savings for the company;
- Participation in a certification programme can provide better access to modern techniques, technology and know-how;
- Applying effective environmental management can help to protect the environmental and cultural assets upon which the tourism industry depends for its continued prosperity.

Finally, certification and ecolabels can of course benefit consumers by providing them with more information and guidance for their decisions on travel choices, as well as assurances for product and service quality.

Recommendations

Certification systems for sustainable tourism need to be developed and operated to fit geographical, political, socio-economic and sectoral characteristics of each country. For this reason, the following recommendations serve as general orientation and they need to be adapted to the economic, institutional, social and environmental conditions prevailing in each country.

1. Development of the Certification System

Governments can play a key role in the initiation and development of certification systems for sustainable tourism by creating the supportive legal and institutional structures. The following general recommendations can be made:

1. Consider a national certification system as an integral part of sustainable tourism development policies, strategies and objectives, and an effective tool to implement them.
2. Identify key stakeholders and potential target groups relèvant to and interested in certification programmes.
3. Develop the certification system through multi-stakeholder consultation processes, involving all relevant interest groups, such us different government authorities (tourism, environment, transportation, finance, education, etc); tourism trade associations and other private groups; academic, education and research institutions; NGOs; consumer associations; etc. The development and the operation of a successful certification program in many cases lays in the multi-stakeholder representation of the team awarding certificates and supporting the program.
4. Coordinate an in-depth research on the conditions and feasibility of a certification system, including aspects such as:

- Existing legal and voluntary instruments affecting the tourism sector (e.g. laws, regulations, taxes, subsidies, local certification systems, codes of conduct, environmental awards, etc.);
- Experience of certification systems applied in other sectors in the country, like agriculture, forestry, and draw lessons from them for the tourism sector

- Certification criteria (see section 2 below);
- Operational mechanisms: application, verification, awarding, revision and inspection procedures; consulting and technical assistance for participants, marketing and communication; funding (see section 3 below).

5. Provide finance and/or seek partners for co-financing and providing technical contributions for the research, development and operational costs of certification programmes (e.g. different government departments, NGOs, academic institutions, international finance and development agencies, private foundations, etc).
6. Ensure transparency throughout all the stages of the development and operation of the certification system and establish an appeals process.
7. Make clear to the private sector the benefits, costs and other implications of certification systems.
8. Develop incentives to motivate and encourage tourism companies to become certified, e.g. marketing incentives by giving priority in trade shows and nationally sponsored publicity, or ensuring access to environmental technologies, etc.
9. Consider issues affecting the sustainability of destinations as a whole, involving all tourism product and service providers.
10. Pay special attention to equitable access to certification, especially by small and medium size firms, as they can have more difficulties in

meeting the costs and technical requirements than bigger companies.

11. Conduct pilot projects for testing and demonstration of the certification system.
12. Prepare the market for certification, in order to reach a good demand level from tourism companies, and a critical mass at the initial phase to get the system running.

2. Certification Criteria

Developing certification criteria is a critical part of the certification system development process. The following general recommendations need to be considered:

1. Base criteria on existing legal standards and instruments and set them well above legal compliance.
2. Include the precondition of compliance by the applicant with these legislations.
3. Address the three dimensions of sustainability: environmental, socio-cultural and economic issues.
4. Define core criteria and supplementary criteria specific for different tourism product and service groups (e.g. hotels and other accommodations, transportation services, restaurants, tour operators and travel agents, attractions, etc.). By this way consider the implications to destinations as a whole, and not just certain tourism product and service groups.
5. In bigger countries, criteria can be adjusted to specific regional and local environmental and socio-economic conditions.

6. For each criterion, define indicators that are measurable and easy to understand by the different type of stakeholders involved in the certification process.
7. Base criteria and indicators on scientific research that evaluates the key environmental and socio-economic impacts of the sector.
8. Criteria should refer to attainable and realistic goals for private sector participants.
9. Criteria can be set in different levels of requirements: from more easily achievable to very demanding criteria. Thus, the certification system sets a framework for continuous improvement whereby applicants can achieve higher performance levels step by step.
10. Compliance with criteria can be measured through process and performance-based assessments. Indicators are essential tools for measuring environmental, social and economic impacts of tourism operations:

    Environmental indicators can relate to the following factors, among others:

    - Environmental impact assessment conducted for setting up the operation or construction of establishments;
    - Environmental management practices, company policies and technical measures (e.g. energy, water saving and waste treatment devices, environmental friendly transportation, etc.) in place;
    - Land use and property issues in destinations;

- Health and safety;
- Use of natural resources:

- Energy (consumption, reduction, efficiency)
- Water (consumption, reduction, quality)
- Solid and liquid waste (reduction, reuse, recycling, treatment, disposal)
- Appropriate building materials
- Hazardous substances (reduction, handling, use of nature friendly cleaning products)
- Noise (reduction)
- Air quality (quality, improvement)
- Habitat/eco-system/wildlife maintenance and enhancement;
  - Environmental information/ interpretation/education for customers;
  - Transportation services (public transport, environmental friendly alternatives;
  - Indicators and standards on the impacts at specific tourist use areas (e.g. beaches) and on the impacts caused by specific tourism activities and facilities (e.g. diving, golf, marinas etc.);
  - Visual impacts of establishments and infrastructure; etc.

Social indicators can relate to the following factors, among others:

- Social impact assessment conducted for setting up the operation and the establishments;

- Staff policies and management (information, education, training, incentives, health, safety, etc.);
- Relationships with local communities (local employees, outreach and education programmes);
- Emphasis on, and conservation of local/ regional culture, heritage and authenticity;
- Maintaining aesthetics of physical development/architecture;
- Community feedback systems, satisfaction of local population;
- Contribution to community development purposes (infrastructure improvement; social services, etc.);
- Information provided to guests on sustainability aspects;
- Guest feedback systems in place, customer satisfaction, etc.

Economic indicators can relate to the following factors, among others:

- Creation of local employment (number of employees from local communities and their level of skills);
- Supply chain management through green and sustainable purchasing policies;
- Creation of networks of environmentally friendly businesses within a given destination;
- Responsible marketing;

- Use of locally sourced and produced materials and food, etc.

In addition, certification criteria for ecotourism should specifically address the elements below, besides the general sustainability criteria:

- Financial and in-kind contributions to conservation of ecotourism sites by companies;
- Level of involvement of local communities and benefits accruing to them;
- Use of specialized guides and other interpretation techniques, information provided to tourists through ecotourism operations;
- Environmental education activities provided for tourists and local populations;
- Locally appropriate scale and design for lodging, infrastructure and tours;
- Minimal impact on and the appropriate presentation of local and indigenous culture.

11. Indicators to measure the success of certification systems can address:
    - The number of applications and certified companies (i.e. increase over time of the number of companies registered in a certain certification system);
    - The percentage of certified companies in the different tourism product and service groups;

- Improvement in environmental and social performance in certified companies (e.g. changes in water and energy consumption, resource savings, etc.);
- Environmental and social performance of certified companies as compared to non-certified ones (e.g. a current estimate is that environmental performance per certified accommodation enterprises can be taken as about 20 % better than the average performance at accommodation facilities in Europe).

12. Consider the whole product life cycle when setting product environmental criteria (from the manufacturing, transporting, through purchasing, consumption, to recycling, disposal, etc.).
13. Undertake periodic revision and update of criteria (e.g. every 2-3 years).

3. Operation of Certification Systems

The procedure is normally composed of the application, verification and certification processes. The funding mechanism for the above services and procedures is a crucial and critical element for the success of certification systems. Normally there is a funding, verification and certification body interacting in these processes. In many cases the funding and certification bodies coincide. Fundamental components of any certification system are the facilitation of consulting, advisory and technical assistance and marketing services. The following general recommendations can be made in relation to the operational processes:

3.1 Application

1. The system should be open to all potential applicants.
2. Provide clear and easily accessible information on the criteria, costs and benefits and other conditions of certification (e.g. through Internet, email, telephone, information kit).
3. Offer immediate sources for consultation services.
4. Show tangible benefits for applicants (e.g costs savings, marketing advantage, access to technical assistance and modern technology and financial possibilities, etc.) and explain clearly the commitments and costs.
5. Application documents should be clear, easy to understand and fill in.
6. Conduct a pre-evaluation/assessment of the applicant in order to identify technical and technological aspects that need to be improved to meet the criteria. Provide assistance and financial incentives for these improvements.

3.2 Verification

7. Verification of compliance with criteria should be done by an independent or third-party organization. In other words by a body which is independent from the parties being certified and of technical assessment or funding.
8. Verification is normally done through a combination of different activities: review of application documents and references, self-assessment by the operation through questionnaire, on-site visit, fees to be paid by the applicant.

9. Verification audits should be conducted by suitably trained auditors.
10. The verification process can be also used to give recommendations to the applicants on how to improve their performance and achieve further progress.

3.3 Certification (awarding of certification)

The certification is basically the awarding of the certification to the applicant, granting a permit for using the logo, marketing and other services of the system.

11. Certification bodies can be composed of representatives of the mayor stakeholder groups participating in the development and operation of the system. Governments have a key role in certification bodies, by giving credibility and recognition of the system.
12. As it was also mentioned among the recommendations for criteria development, awarding of certification can be done at single-level or at multi-level. The latter one occurs if criteria are set on different scales with a view to ensure a framework of continuous improvement.
13. The certification, the use of a logo and related benefits should be granted for a pre-determined period, after which re-assessment and verification should be conducted to ensure continuous compliance with the same or higher criteria.
14. Follow up control can be conducted after certification. For example, the WTO study on voluntary initiatives demonstrated that more than 50% of the certification systems currently

operating undertake some control visits after certification: 38% are announced, and 17% are surprise visits. Some eco-labels either do phone checks, stimulating guests' feedback or sending "mystery guests" to the certified tourism service.

15. Procedures have to be in place for the cancellation and withdrawal of certification and the use of the corresponding logo in case of non-compliance.
16. The certification system can also include consumer and local community feedback mechanisms.

3.4 Consulting, Advisory and Technical Assistance Services

The facilitation of the following services represents important added value for tourism companies and can be decisive factors for joining the certification system.

17. Provide technical consultancy options from the initial expression of interest and through the application phases onward, and give guidance to the applicant at every stage of the process.
18. Facilitate technical assistance for applicants so that they can introduce advanced management techniques and technology to meet the certification criteria. Provide access to environmental technologies, equipments and techniques by creating alliances with other organizations that can provide assistance for this purpose.
19. Develop training and capacity building programmes in form of courses, workshops, distance learning, etc.
20. Organize regular meetings for certified companies to promote the exchange of experiences and the sense of group.

21. Constant assistance and advisory is especially important in certification systems where the criteria and awarding are set on different scales.

3.5 Marketing and Communication

Marketing is another fundamental element of certification programmes, representing perhaps the biggest attraction and the most tangible benefits for private companies. The following general recommendations can be made:

22. Develop a precise marketing strategy for the certification system targeting three groups in principle:
    - 22.1 Potential candidates: aiming at attracting companies to join the programme
    - 22.2 Applicants and certified companies: providing marketing and promotional support and market advantages for them
    - 22.3 Consumers: reaching recognition of the certification programmes, fostering responsible travel choices, and make effective the marketing advantage for certified companies.
23. Develop a well-distinguished and unequivocal logo design for the system. The logo can be accompanied by a motto, or slogan. Ensure legal protection of the logo.
24. The presentation of the system in media and communication should reflect a well recognized corporate image in the market for businesses and consumers as well. The system can represent a sort of brand.

25. Use all available forms and channels to publicize and provide information on the certification programme for companies and consumers (e.g. brochures, flyers, guide books, printed and electronic media, Internet, conferences, seminars, tourism and trade fairs, etc.)
26. Give good media coverage to the awarding ceremonies.
27. Provide marketing support and promotion for certified companies through national tourist boards or national tourism marketing organizations, e.g. presentation of these companies in national brochures, catalogues, listings, websites, support for presence at national stands at tourism fairs and exhibition, etc.
28. Give recommendations and examples to applicants and certified companies on how to include the certificate in their own marketing activities.
29. Demonstrate the distinction on environmental performance, economic and socio-cultural effects between certified and non-certified products/ companies.
30. Communicate on a regular basis with certified members (e.g. through periodic meetings and events, newsletters, emails, exclusive access to information on Internet, etc.)
31. Provide clear and easily understandable information to consumers on the characteristics and added value that certification represents.
32. Develop consumer awareness raising and education campaigns on the certification system and certified products.

33. Involve consumer associations in these efforts

3.6 Fees and Funding

Governments have a key role in providing funding themselves, and/or in conceiving and developing alternative funding mechanisms with other partners for the operation of the certification system.

34. Establish the right balance between financial contributions of the public and private sectors.
35. Ensure that the sources of funding do not create a conflict of interest, since undue influence by funding organizations should be avoided in the certification procedure.
36. Establish fees for participants to cover (at least part of) application and verification costs. Fees should be kept as low as possible in order to encourage participation.
37. Fees should be calculated proportionally to size of businesses (e.g. by number of beds or visitors, turnover, etc.).
38. Provide incentive measures and support the application of companies, especially of small and medium size enterprises that would otherwise be left out (e.g. by soft loans and subsidies to make the necessary improvements to meet the criteria).
39. Consider in-kind contributions by governments for the operation, e.g. providing facilities, office space and equipment.

Final Note: Governments are encouraged to convey to the World Tourism Organization their experience in connection with certification systems related to sustainability in tourism. This will allow WTO to periodically revise these guidelines, introduce any additional guidelines or modify those recommended above (Madrid, March 2003).

APPENDICES

APPENDIX—1

DECLARATIONS ON SUSTAINABLE TOURISM

Appendix J. Council of Europe
[Recommendation No. R (94) 7]

On a General Policy for Sustainable and Environment-Friendly Tourism Development.

The Committee of Ministers, under the terms of Article 15 (b) of the Statute of the Council of Europe;

Considering that the aim of the organisation is to achieve a greater unity between its members, inter alia in order to foster their economic and social progress;

Having regard to the various activities carried out within the Council of Europe and other international organisations;

Bearing in mind the declaration of the ministerial conference held in Lucerne from 28 to 30 April 1993 on "Environment for Europe", which calls on the Council of Europe to pursue its activities to promote ecologically viable tourism;

Taking into account the declaration of the United Nations Conference on Environment and Development held in Rio from 3 to 14 June 1992;

Stressing that tourism constitutes one of the mainsprings of economic growth and is likely to become the foremost world industry;

Acknowledging that tourism is a factor in bringing people together, forging a European identity and heightening awareness of the value of their natural and cultural heritage;

Noting a growing interest in all forms of tourism associated with the discovciy and knowledge of the natural and cultural heritage;

As a tourism asset;

Underlining that the relationship between tourism and the environment is a delicate one;

Aware of the threats posed to the natural and landscape environment and local populations and cultures by the excessive and uncontrolled development of tourism;

Observing that levels of tourism development and fragility of the areas concerned vary from one country to another, and even from one region to another;

Convinced of the need to establish a general framework in order to safeguard and restore the quality of the environment, which is the prime resource of tourism.

Recommends that the governments of member states:

(a) base their tourism development policy on the principles and measures set out in the appendix to this recommendation, tailoring them where necessary to the special features or fragility of certain regions;

(b) ensure that the national, regional and local authorities, those institutions responsible for tourism and the environment, the tourist industry and all other sectors involved be duly informed of this recommendation and respect the principles contained herein.

Instructs the Secretary General to convey this recommendation to the international organisations and international financial bodies working in the field of the development of tourism.

Appendix to Recommendation No. R (94) 7

I. General Principles

1. The principles of prevention, precaution and remedial action allied with the need for sustainable development should underlie any tourism development policy.

2. Every planned tourism activity or development should be geared to sustainable development and its impact on the environment should be assessed; environmental considerations should be integrated into the decision-making process from the start of the project.

3. In principle, no permission should be given for any project having a significant environmental impact without evidence of its environmental, economic and financial viability. However, if this cannot be proven, other considerations may be taken into account, such as the projects contribution to socio-cultural development.

4. Tourism development should be totally or partly self-financing where possible, with the emphasis on achieving or building on sustainability.

5. Tourism development should be a gradual process and not outstrip infrastructure improvements. Tourism projects must be carried out within the limits of the local infrastructure.

6. Tourism should be developed so that in addition it benefits the local community, provides support for the local economy and takes account of the latter's ability to absorb development. Wherever possible, it should encourage employment of the local workforce and use local materials and traditional skills.

7. Tourism activities and amenities should be located in carefully chosen areas so as to restrict development in sensitive regions. Wherever possible, before building any new amenities, the possibility of using, modernising or rehabilitating existing infrastructures should first be considered.

8. Tourism activities and development must respect the scale, nature, character and capacity of the local physical and social environment of the place in which they are sited, as well as its natural resources, landscape quality, historic and archaeological heritage and cultural identity.

To this end, every project should be subjected to an environmental impact assessment Where an environmental impact assessment (ELA) is required, due to the nature and size of the project and the character of the area to be affected, the following elements should be included:

- the impact on environment, landscape, fauna, flora, water, land and energy resources;
- the impact on local infrastructure, economy, society and employment;

- the direct, indirect, immediate and long-term effects of the project;
- the effects of secondary developments (transport, new infrastructures, etc.);
- adequate consultation with the local public and local communities;
- possible remedial or compensating measures.

9. Therefore, where appropriate, every tourism project should:

- avoid creating additional pressures on the environment;
- encourage the use of public and non-motorised transport, us well as the most suitable technology for saving water and energy, treating effluent and processing and recycling waste;
- be accompanied by a monitoring programme to ensure that once in operation, the project keeps to its environmental commitments, and that unforeseen negative impacts are detected and dealt with immediately. Eco-audits should be carried out on large-scale developments;
- strive to make visitors aware of the need to protect the environment and the constraints that this protection entails.

II. Implementation of the General Principles

The implementation of the general principles will be at international, national, regional and local level.

A. National Authorities

1. In order to implement the general principles national authorities should:

(a) develop national strategies for sustainable and environmentally friendly development;

(b) ensure that the various policies and decision-making levels are coherent and consistent. Tourism development is to be considered in terms of both the overall economy of a country ami the local economy;

(c) attempt to draw up an inventory of the country's cultural and natural resources and set up a legislative framework to enhance and protect them where necessary;

(d) preserve areas designated as vulnerable by following a policy of land use control and through purchase, renting and management agreements;

(e) draw up a framework for integrated planning and resource management;

(f) draw up a national tourism policy taking full account of the environment and defining the role and importance of tourism in the national economy; such a policy should be tied in with overall planning policy;

(g) ensure close collaboration between bodies responsible for providing reliable statistics on the tourist industry and monitoring the state of the country's environment;

(h) provide environmental education and training for tourism professionals and ensure that training in the tourism sector builds awareness of the environment;

(i) run campaigns to build awareness of the environment among local communities, elected representatives in tourist destinations and tourists themselves;

(j) propose charters for the tourist industry establishing qualitative criteria for environmentally friendly tourism;

(k) control tourist demand and flow, in particular by staggering the tourist season and easing pressure on certain sites by developing other centres of interest, introducing admission fees at certain sites or for certain services, or limiting the number of tourists;

(l) ensure that sites harmed by excessive tourism are restored as appropriate;

(m) diversify what is on offer for tourists by encouraging new types of activities as alternatives to mass tourism, based on an interest in the country concerned and knowledge of its heritage, culture and way of life;

(n) encourage the introduction of environmentally sound products and activities by relevant measures including the awarding of prizes and quality labels;

(o) consider, where appropriate, the development of a tax incentive scheme to encourage environment -friendly tourism development projects;

2. National authorities, acting through international organisations, should propose that these organisations:

(a) adopt an integrated planning approach to future development of the tourism industry, emphasising the need to protect the social, natural and cultural environments;

(b) promote international awards for sustainable tourism respecting the environment;

(c) publish international guides of good tourism practice vis-a-vis the environment, including databases of relevant documents and successful projects;

(d) support training and awareness-building programmes on tourism and the environment;

(e) support pilot projects for sustainable tourism and disseminate information about them.

3. National authorities, acting through international financial bodies, should propose that these bodies:

(a) request environmental impact statements for all projects they finance and run impact assessment studies (EIA) themselves where appropriate;

(b) ensure that all relevant procedures have been complied with;

(c) ascertain the environmental viability of the project on the same footing as the economic and financial viability of the project;

(d) make suitable supervision arrangements to check that the project is properly run;

(e) encourage the use of the most appropriate technology so as to minimise the impact on the environment.

B. Local and Regional Authorities

In order to implement the general principles local and regional authorities should:

(a) exercise control over tourist development with potentially significant environmental consequences through regional, local and urban planning policy and a policy of nature and landscape protection;

(b) establish local tourism plans, based on inventories of sites and biotopes and on their carrying capacity and social accommodation capacity as well as land use plans; local tourism plans should be integrated into overall local development plans, and local tourism development funding should be provided in the framework of these plans where appropriate;

(c) make the issue of building permits contingent on requirements such as a guarantee of quality development and respect for the environment, and ensure that these criteria are respected;

(d) work closely with all public and private-sector operators to ensure co-ordination between different tourism development projects, and maintain a regular, two way flow of information.

APPENDIX—2

MALE' DECLARATION ON SUSTAINABLE TOURISM DEVELOPMENT

Adopted at the Asia-Pacific Ministers' Conference on Tourism and Environment — (Male', Maldives, 16th February, 1997)

Whereas the Asia-Pacific Tourism Ministers' Conference on Tourism and Environment was held on 16th February 1997, in Male', Republic of Maldives, convened by the World Tourism Organization with the participation of delegations of 25 States, Affiliate Members, international organizations, regional organizations and observers, to clarify and define the linkage between tourism and environment, as well as to consider the responsibility of States and the private sector for achieving a high degree of sustainable tourism development;

Whereas the theme of the conference, 'Tourism 2000—Building a Sustainable Future for Asia-Pacific", attests to the unanimous sentiment on the part of the conference participants that tourism can and should promote environmental health and integrity, and that the substantial and ongoing investment of financial, human, and natural resources in tourism development requires a fiduciary responsibility to the sustainability and continued viability of the industry for the benefit of communities and nations; and

Whereas there is recognition and appreciation for the uniqueness and diversity of natural environments, peoples, cultures, and heritages of the Asia-Pacific countries and their importance for tourism's potential for cross-cultural learning, international understanding, and world peace; and

Whereas the conference participants have explored the many policy-related and technical issues involved in sustainability, with an emphasis on those of particular relevance to the public sector; now, therefore,

Be it resolved by conference that the participants of the Asia-Pacific Ministers' Conference on Tourism and Environment agree in principle to:

Pledge continuing support for the vision and goals of a sustainable future, as conceived and articulated in the 1987 Brundtland Commission report, the 1992 Earth Summit, the Rio Declaration, and Agenda 21, and further extended to the tourism industry through subsequent efforts such as Agenda 21 for the Travel and Tourism Industry, the World Conference on Sustainable Tourism, and the 1996 International Conference on Tourism and Heritage Management, encompassing the following precepts:

- Fostering awareness of environmental ethics in tourism among communities and consumers;
- Conservation and sustainable use of resources;
- Public guardianship of the natural environment;
- Reducing consumption and waste;
- Natural, social and cultural diversity;
- Integrated tourism planning for sustainability;
- Support for local economies;
- Local community involvement;
- Consulting tourism stakeholders and the public;
- Human resource development;
- Responsible tourism marketing;
- Ongoing inquiry into sustainability issues;

- Measurements to monitor tourism's impacts on environment, culture and heritage; and
- Use of environmental impact assessments in tourism planning.

Commit resources to environmental protection and to improving the quality and professionalism of our human resources to create a valuable and meaningful visitor experience and to meet the needs of a competitive global environment;

Emphasize the urgency of sustainability for the health of both the tourism industry and the world economy, and especially for vulnerable ecosystems such as small island states;

Intensify efforts to make operational those policies and practices that promote sustainability, including further refinement of sustainable indicators to measure progress, realizing that research and technological advances have brought us to the point where sustainable action can now proceed;

Strive to provide the leadership, training, and technical support needed by communities to enable them to become fully aware of, and involved with, the processes by which tourism is planned and developed;

Support an active and prominent role for governments at all levels— national, provincial and local—in planning and promoting sustainable development;

Seek greater international and regional cooperation among Asian-Pacific nations in collaborating on sustainable tourism programs and sharing resources, expertise and information on best practices and experiences;

Call on the WTO and other appropriate bodies to expand the base of knowledge on sustainability issues, problems, and solutions for achieving sustainable balance;

Strengthen and promote cooperation with the many tourism-related businesses and organizations that comprise the private and nongovernmental sectors, in recognition of the costs and effort that sustainability requires for optimizing opportunities; and

Be it finally resolved that the participants urge their governments to use the principles of this Declaration as a policy tool to measure progress towards sustainability and to assist in the implementation of sustainable practices.

APPENDIX—3

ECOLOGICAL TOURISM IN EUROPE (E.T.E.)

The society was founded in Bonn, Germany, in 1991 as a forum for national organisations supporting environmentally and socially responsible tourism. Currently E.T.E. has six member organisations, which work in the fields of nature and environmental protection, tourism, youth, leisure and culture, and alternative forms of transportation.

E.T.E. has set itself the following tasks and goals:

- Offering specific information and education about environmentally friendly and sustainable forms of tourism to providers of tourism services and tourists
- Initiating, supporting and carrying out of model projects designed to promote environmentally friendly and socially responsible tourism
- Political and administrative lobbying
- Initiating and implementing an environmental award scheme for the national tourism industry

In co-operation with other organisations, mainly from the nature and environmental conservation sectors, E.T.E. carries out regional model projects designed to promote environmentally and socially sustainable tourism as a basis for or support of sustainable regional development in Germany and other European countries. The organisers of one of these projects, which promotes a sustainable regional tourism initiative in Gomorszis, Hungary, were recently awarded the British Airways Tourism for Tomorrow Award, the Council of Europe's Landscape Award and the national

Kos-Karoly-Award for maintaining the built and natural environment. It is because of these regional projects that E.T.E. has broad and sound practical experience in the subject area of environmentally and socially responsible tourism, in particular concerning the needs for collaboration between the various actors on local level. Moreover, E.T.E.'s public relations activities allow for the permanent representation of interests on the subject of environmentally and socially responsible tourism in the public, political and administrative sectors. It also provides specific information for tourists interested in environmental issues. E.T.E. also organises conferences, expert meetings, information events, seminars and workshops both on the national and international levels. Since 1998, E.T.E. has been continuously working on international level on the tourism issue within the Commission for Sustainable Development and the Convention on Biological Diversity. In both processes, E.T.E. supports the "International Guidelines for Sustainable Tourism". E.T.E. is supported by a regular team of experts from the environmental and tourism sectors (some are self-employed, some work for one of the member organisations). The experts are integrated into the work of E.T.E. according to individual project needs. In Germany, E.T.E. is a leading expert group in the environmental sector, working with others on initiating and implementing an environmental award scheme for the national tourism industry.

APPENDIX—4

BONN ENVIRONMENTAL DECLARATION ON . TOURISM

Bundesverband der Deutschen Tourismuswirtschaft e.V. (BTW) Federal Association of the German Tourism Industry

Bundesverband Deutscher Omnibusunternehmer e.V. (bdo) Federal Association of German Coach and Bus Operators

Bundesverband mittelstandischer Reiseunternehmen e.V. (asr) Federal Association of Independent Travel Agencies and Tour Operators

Deutsche Zentrale fur Tourismus e.V. (DZT)

German National Tourist Board

Deutscher Baderverband e.V. (DBV)

German Spa Association

Deutsche; Fremdenverkehrsverband e.V. (DFV)

German Tourist Association

Deutscher Hotel- und Gaststattenverband e.V. (DEHOGA)

German Hotel and Restaurant Association

Deutscher Reiseburo-Verband e.V. (DRV)

German Travel Agents' and Tour Operators' Association

Internationaler Bustouristik Verband e.V. (RDA)

International Federation of Coach Tourism

This Environmental Declaration was adopted by the following central associations organisations of the German tourism industry:

Bundesverband der Deutschen Tourismuswirtschaft e.V. (BTW), Bonn Federal Association of the German Tourism Industry

Bundesverband Deutscher Omnibusunternehmer e.V. (bdo), Bonn Federal Association of German Coach and Bus Operators

Bundesverband mittelstandischer Reiseunternehmen e.V. (asr), Frankfurt/Main Federal Association of Independent Travel Agencies and Tour Operators

Deutsche Zentrale fur Tourismus e.V. (DZT), Frankfurt/ Main German National Tourist Board

Deutscher Baderverband e.V. (DBV), Bonn Gentian Spa Association

Deutscher Fremdenverkehrsverband e.V. (DFV), Bonn German Tourist Association

Deutscher Hotel- und Gaststattenverband e.V. (DEHOGA), Bonn German Hotel and Restaurant Association

Deutscher Reiseburo-Verband e.V. (DRV), Frankfurt/ Main German Travel Agents' and Tour Operators' Association

Internationaler Bustouristik Verband e.V. (RDA), Koln International Federation of Coach Tourism

with the support of

the Federal Ministry for the Environment, Nature Conservation and Nuclear Safety

and the Federal Ministry of Economics

and scientific assistance from

DWIF - Deutsches Wirtschaftswissenschaftliches Institut fur Fremdenverkehr e.V.

an der Universitat Munchen e. V. (DWIF)

German Economic Science Institute for Tourism at the University of Munich

DWIF's Berlin Office Werderstrabe 14, 12105 Berlin

Bonn, October 1997.

I. Preamble

A healthy environment and unspoiled nature have always constituted the most important foundation for tourism. Clean air, clear, uncontaminated water and attractive natural scenery are vital prerequisites for tourism's long-term viability. This has long been understood by the industry's associations and companies, which are engaged in a wide variety of activities designed to promote environmentally appropriate tourism. The possibility of climate change, the threat to biodiversity and sensitive ecosystems and the pollution of seas and coasts, not to mention the many other burdens on nature and landscapes that exist in many tourism regions, are increasingly endangering the very existence of our industry. In future we therefore need lifestyles and forms of economic activity that reflect the finite character of natural resources and the need to protect nature and the environment, and thereby contribute to the preservation of the natural foundations of human life for both present and future generations. This is only possible through a common effort on the part of all forces in society. Industries associations and companies, policymakers and consumers are all called upon to play their part. And tourism, as the world's largest single industry and a major branch of the German economy, bears great responsibility alongside others.

Aware of:

1. the manifold risks and opportunities associated with tourism development;

2. the need to protect humankind, the environment, nature and culture in tourist destinations;
3. the fact that, as a major source country of outgoing tourism, Germany has a particular duty to promote sustainable, ecologically sound development at home and abroad;
4. the special responsibility for acting in the interest of human health to safeguard the natural curative powers of the soil, the climate and the sea against environmental damage;
5. the sovereign right of the inhabitants of tourism regions to determine how tourism develops and to participate in planning processes;
6. the growing experience as travellers and increasing environmental sensitivity on the part of German and foreign tourists,

the central associations of the German tourism industry hereby affirm the necessity of pursuing sustainable development and ecologically responsible policies on tourism.

Economic development and economic growth should serve to improve people's quality of life. By the same token, the development of tourism should only be supported to the extent that it serves to improve the quality of life. Efforts made in connection with business activity to protect and maintain the natural resource base also contribute to securing the future viability of the industry and its businesses. They lead to savings in the use of resources, often creating a variety of cost benefits, and secure the long-term profitability and future of businesses. They enhance product quality and quality awareness, strengthen motivation among the staff of companies and help to attract new, environmentally conscious customers. The central associations and organisations of the German tourism industry recognise their special responsibility for sustainable tourism development. They shall endeavour to intensify cooperation with partners outside the tourism sector.

II. Purpose of the Environmental Declaration

Guided by the objectives and principles contained in the Rio Declaration and Agenda 21 (adopted at Rio de Janeiro in 1992), in Agenda 21 for the Travel and Tourism Industry (World Travel and Tourism Council - WTTC) and in the Charter for Sustainable Tourism (World Conference on Sustainable Tourism - WCST), the central associations of the German tourism industry agree to adopt the present declaration. The present declaration builds on existing environmental statements, resolutions and a variety of ecological measures already effected by the undersigned associations and their members. The undersigned associations and organisations resolve that this environmental declaration shall serve as a guideline for the future activities and efforts of the various institutions of the German tourism industry to achieve sustainable development. It shall also serve as a basis for greater consolidation and coordination of activities by the industry's associations and organisations in the field of environmental protection and nature conservation.

III. Definition of Sustainable Tourism

Development is sustainable if it "meets the needs of the present without compromising the ability of future generations to meet their own needs." (Brundtland Report, 1987). Sustainable development should lead to an improvement in mankind's living conditions without exerting excessive burdens on the ecosystems. In other words, the use of a resource must not in the long run exceed its capacity for regeneration, while the emission of substances and energy must not exceed the capacity of environmental media to withstand burdens or assimilate to changes. Economic development must in future be accompanied by ongoing reductions in the consumption of resources. Sustainable development is a comprehensive system of objectives that treats environmental protection and nature conservation as an integral part of all relevant decision-making processes in society. Tourism must, in the long term, be made both ecologically and economically viable as well as ethically and socially acceptable. The maintenance of life-supporting ecological processes and natural life-cycles, the conservation of biological diversity and the low-impact utilisation of natural resources must therefore be regarded as objectives of tourism in the same way as respect for and preservation of traditional ways of life and people's cultural identity worldwide. The objectives, content and measures required for sustainable development must be elaborated jointly by all stakeholders. The tourism industry shall therefore cooperate with other social forces, including government, associations, other branches of industry, non-governmental organisations and local communities. The equally crucial task of implementation should centre on solutions based on voluntary commitments by producers and service providers working together with consumers. Their commitments must also reflect their global responsibilities. The central associations and organisations of German tourism regard sustainable tourism as a fundamental objective for the future development of the industry.

IV. Main Tasks of Individual Central Associations and Organisations and Their Special Responsibility

The central associations and the businesses or institutions

they represent operate in different segments of the tourism market. Consequently they have different responsibilities with regard to achieving sustainable development. The tourism regions, towns and communities in general and health resorts, spas and their spa establishments in particular are responsible for the municipal and regional tourism services on offer within Germany. They are represented by the Deutscher Fremdenverkehrsverband e.V. (DFV; German Tourist Association) and the Deutscher Baderverband e.V. (DBV; German Spa Association). The hoteliers and caterers, who constitute the most important group of commercial service provider in tourism locations and regions, are represented by the Deutscher Hotel- und Gaststattenverband e.V. (DEHOGA; German Hotel and Restaurant Association). Together, the two groups represent the key providers for domestic tourism in Germany. They also play the key role in determining what tourist opportunities are available to (incoming) foreign, guests. Tourism regions and locations as well as the hotel and restaurant trade therefore have a responsibility for developing Germany into a travel destination characterised by sustainable, environmentally appropriate tourism and, above all, for preserving the natural resource base required for the health and recuperation of their visitors. In its role as a marketing organisation, the Deutsche Zentrale fur Tourismus e.V. (DZT; German National Tourist Board) promotes Germany as a travel and holiday destination and advertises abroad the range of tourism services offered by German providers. As part of its sales promotion effort the DZT places special emphasis on the environmentally oriented holidays on offer. It also keeps tourism service providers informed of foreign demand for environmentally relevant tourism products. Operating in the spirit of international partnership, the DZT is able to foster know-how transfer and information exchange between German and foreign tourism organisations, policy-making bodies, government authorities and the service providers, above all in developing countries. Tour operators and travel agencies assemble and sell holidays at home and abroad on behalf of German tourists. They are represented by the Deutscher Reiseburo-Verband e.V. (DRV; German Travel Agents' and Tour Operators' Association) and the Bundesverband mittelstandischer Reiseunternehmen e.V. (asr; Federal Association of Independent Travel Agencies and Tour Operators). In performing their role as coordinators, packagers and mediators between German consumers, municipal and commercial service providers and other tourism-related businesses (carriers, insurers etc.), they support sustainable development in the tourist destinations. They inform consumers, raise awareness of ecological problems and promote the environmentally sound design and composition of travel products. Companies in the tourism sector that operate internationally have a special responsibility with regard to sustainable tourism in foreign destinations, above all in developing countries. The Bundesverband der Deutschen Tourismuswirtschaft e.V. (BTW; Federal Association of the German Tourism Industry) draws together the strengths of its individual members and represents their views to policy-makers and other sectors of the economy. Working together with the relevant political institutions, the BTW seeks to create the best possible framework for achieving sustainable development in tourism. Most of Germany's private bus and coach companies are important providers of tourism services as tour operators and as excursion and coach hire businesses. They take special account of the requirements of ecologically favourable tourist mobility. The Bundesverband Deutscher Omnibusunternehmer e.V. (bdo; Federal Association of

German Coach and Bus Operators) and the Internationaler Bustouristik Verband e.V. (RDA; International Federation of Coach Tourism) are the umbrella organisations of the private coach and bus sector.

The central associations and organisations of the German tourism industry resolve to continue to fulfil their special responsibilities for environmental protection and nature conservation. To this end, they shall strengthen cooperation both among themselves and with other partners of relevance to tourism.

V. Guidelines for Sustainable Development in Tourism

1. Creating and Evaluating Framework Conditions. The principle of precautionary action to safeguard the environment must be applied more forcefully at all levels and in all fields. Only if practical framework conditions are put into place, will it be possible to achieve sustainable development in tourism. The associations representing the tourism industry are in favour of establishing the best possible combination of regulatory, economic and voluntary instruments by working together with the competent authorities and ministries. Wherever possible voluntary measures should be given preference over cumbersome rules and regulations. Economic policy instruments should be employed and developed in such a way that negative environmental impacts can be avoided. This demands Europe-wide and even global harmonisation of the general legal and economic conditions. Greater assistance should in future be given to sustainable tourism projects. The tourism industry shall employ and actively promote environmental management systems and other market-based instruments along with measures such as competitions, pilot projects, environmental seals of approval and criteria, and advisory and information initiatives. In addition, the eco-audit system should be implemented in appropriate areas. Any differences or contradictions between the objectives of policy-makers and industry associations with respect to sustainable development in tourism shall be clearly identified so that they can be resolved as far as possible. Environment policy goals and measures that apply outside the tourism sector but nevertheless affect or benefit tourism must be adjusted to facilitate sustainable tourism.

2. *Establishing and Consolidating Environmental Management and Environmentally Conscious Organisational Structures.* To succeed in creating the necessary orientation towards sustainable development in tourism, it is necessary to establish and develop environmentally oriented organisational structures in the associations, in the policy-making arena and in other social spheres. Moreover, environmental management must be introduced in businesses. In this way, environmental protection and nature conservation should become an integral part of all the relevant decision-making processes in tourism companies and organisations. Appropriate organisational structures shall be developed and used in accordance with the size and structure of the respective companies and associations. Suitable measures to establish environmentally oriented organisational structures shall include the appointment of environment protection officers and environmental committees, the incorporation of environmental protection and nature conservation in statutes, the elaboration of declarations on environmental protection and environmental policies or codes of conduct for companies, sectors of industry and associations. In this respect, the tourism industry regards the plans to extend the scope of the EU Eco-audit Regulation (EMAS) to cover the service sector as a useful instrument for relevant spheres of tourism.

3. Environmentally Appropriate Planning. Environmentally appropriate planning shall include the implementation of environmental impact assessments for large-scale tourism projects, the appraisal of their effects on infrastructure, the designing of models for regional and local evaluation and guidelines for environmentally appropriate development, the assessment of ecological potential as well as working with others in the region to draw up sustainable models and environmentally oriented development concepts. Through far-sighted forward planning the economic and social benefits for the tourism regions can be maximised without destroying the natural and cultural foundations of those benefits. Without appropriate planning and implementation, the ecological and cultural features of tourism areas are likely to suffer degradation. Environmentally favourable planning must take account of the limits of a region's ecological resilience. For this reason service providers and tourism industry associations advocate sustainable development planning. The local communities and local governments should be involved in the planning process and given an equal vote so that their interests can be properly taken into account and the potential of a region can be used to maximum benefit. In the context of product planning, for example, this entails a deliberate effort to identify employment-generating combinations of economic activities (e.g. exploiting linkages between tourism, forestry, agriculture and craft industries). Land use planning and transport planning are particularly important in this process.

4. Designing and Managing Sustainable Products. The essence of any environmentally appropriate tourism development must be the sustainable design and management of travel and holiday products. The tourism industry is not only seeking the environmental restructuring of intensive forms of tourism, i.e. "mass tourism" and its centres, but also pursuing the sustainable development of nature-centred holidays in the case of extensive forms of tourism (including "eco-tourism"). Sustainability should also lead to enhanced quality and improved competitiveness by means of innovation and diversification of tourism products. Important stepping stones in this direction are company-wide environmental standards and principles for environmentally sound production, the intensification of research and development and the inspection and control of tourism products. Sustainable design and management of tourism products takes place at three levels: first, at the level of the provider of individual lourism services; second, at the level of destinations and locations; and third, in relation to the packaging and combining of products as well as their distribution by tour operators and travel agencies. What characterises developments at the level of the individual tourism establishments is the use of in-house environmental management to implement environmental protection measures. These measures range from green procurement and rational use of resources through to sound disposal practices and environmental information for guests and visitors. Bodies at the regional and local level are responsible for promoting "holistic" tourism and their efforts should be characterised by the detailed elaboration and implementation of sustainable tourism policies and planning measures (sustainable tourism concepts). The key elements here include ascertaining environmental qualities, specifying the capacity limits on the supply of local tourism services, formulating policy on the control of visitor flows and on zoning for nature conservation, identifying historical monuments and cultural heritage sites, and drawing up low-traffic and traffic-reducing schemes. The DFV runs a nationwide competition in Germany ("Environmentally Friendly Tourist Resorts") to encourage this kind of holistic design and management of tourism. Finally, the level of tour operators and travel agencies is characterised by the packaging of individual services to provide environmentally sound holidays. Encouragement shall be given above all to environmentally conscious service providers, ecologically committed destinations, and cleaner forms of mobility. As for their mediating function, these businesses must inform and sensitise not only consumers but also their commercial contracting partners in an effort to develop sustainable tourism products and sustainable consumer behaviour. In striving to create sustainably designed holidays, all stakeholders in tourism shall make a special effort to promote tourism provision that,

(a) helps reduce or avoid burdens on the environment caused by motorised traffic; this applies both to arrangements for low-impact travel to and from destinations and low-impact mobility within the tourism areas.

The most important elements are initiatives to switch from individual motorised transport to rail and bus services, introduce far more fuel-efficient and low-emission transportation, facilitate a reorientation from individual transport to public transport, avoid traffic by promoting integrated transport systems, expand the network of cycleways and footpaths, improve arrangements for taking bicycles on trains and buses, optimise rail and bus services for holiday regions in connection with locally integrated fare and timetable systems, promote regional products and thereby reduce transportation distances, and promote traffic-reduced or car-free health resorts, holiday locations and city centres.

We shall also step up efforts to reduce the environmental burdens caused by air traffic. (carbon dioxide and pollutant emissions, noise)

(b) minimises the consumption of resources, including water, energy and other raw materials, or enhances sustainability by greater use of renewable or regenerative resources.

This is closely linked to the issue of reducing waste and waste-water and ensuring properly managed, environmentally favourable disposal of unavoidable wastes. Hazardous substances are to be substituted wherever possible.

(c) avoids land depletion, is characterised by locally typical and landscape-appropriate building development and promotes the conservation of the landscape's natural features (also in the case of noise abatement structures). Moreover, this will improve the quality of the holidays on offer in centres of mass tourism.

(d) contributes to reducing pressures on ecologically highly sensitive areas (above all nature reserves, vulnerable mountain ecosystems, natural aquatic environments and coastal areas) by controlling visitor flows and by the ecologically appropriate management of leisure activities.

5. Using Tourism to Protect the Environment, Nature and Culture. As the beneficiary and natural ally of a healthy environment, unspoiled nature and intact local culture, the tourism industry is committed to their active conservation. This commitment centres on making use of tourism's potential for giving these resources an economic value that can then become the basis for their protection (upward spiral of benefits). In keeping with this approach, the tourism industry shall support sustainable tourism in large-scale protected areas (national parks, biosphere reserves and wildlife parks) in Germany, as well as in foreign tourism destinations, provided such tourism is compatible with the protection goals. The structures that have historically evolved in regions and landscapes must be strengthened by carefully integrating traditional forms of agriculture, forestry or craft industry into the development of tourism. Steps must be taken to ensure that local communities become economic stakeholders. That above all requires the conservation of historical landscapes by promoting the traditional types of farming. Tourism should be used to upgrade historical monuments, cultural heritage sites, traditional settlement patterns and town centres and to secure their preservation.

6. Promoting National Cooperation and Partnership Between the Tourism Sector, Government Authorities, Non-governmental Organisations, Communities and the Regions. Environmental protection and nature conservation is a joint task for all stakeholders. Sustainable development in tourism can only be achieved in the framework of a functioning partnership between all stakeholders. Acting alone, an organisation, a business or even a government will not achieve the kind of results that can flow from joint action. That is why cross-sectoral cooperation is necessary at every level. An important example of cooperation in tourist destinations is the work done by open tourism fora. It is also important to foster dialogue between different branches of industry, including those outside tourism, wherever this is sensible and feasible. This may take the form of jointly funded initiatives, cooperation between large companies and small and medium-sized enterprises, exchanges of managerial and technological know-how, collaboration with research institutions or other such activities. The tourism associations shall continue to strengthen their important role as mediators, facilitating cooperation between government institutions and industry aimed at sustainable, environmentally appropriate development in tourism.

7. International Exchange of Information, Know-how and Technology Transfer and Partnerships. As one of the main source countries of outgoing tourism, Germany and its tourism industry bear a special responsibility for the necessary exchange of information, the transfer of skills and expertise and cooperation with other countries to create sustainable tourism. Consequently, the industry and in particular internationally operating tourism businesses have a key role to play in systematically promoting the building of global partnerships, especially between industrialised and developing countries. Important elements of global partnership include the provision of information on environmental technology and planning, the launching of partnership programmes, cooperation and information exchange with international organisations, the recognition of best practice through international competitions (e.g. DRV environment prize), joint conferences and seminars, and assistance in procuring finance and funding. The German tourism industry also supports the development of internationally harmonised agreements and arrangements for sustainable development in tourism al global level.

8. Raising Awareness of Tourism-Related Environmental Issues Among Service Providers, Organisations and Travellers. Knowledge and insight are crucial if people are to accept the need for sustainable development in tourism. That is why the industry's central associations and the sectors they represent support the continuous provision of information to educate all interest groups in the travel and tourism industry about the need to develop environmentally appropriate forms of tourism. A special effort must be made to promote environmental awareness among travellers, since in the long run our natural life-support systems can only be maintained if consumption patterns are changed. Thus, marketing must include the dissemination of properly researched customer information on the environmental situation prevailing in tourism destinations and in tourism establishments. This information initiative must be based on environmental criteria that are standardised as far as possible and applied fairly to the destinations, tourism companies and the holidays on offer. Staff must be trained to explain environmental issues to guests in a professional manner. Animators shall endeavour to foster a positive attitude to engaging with nature and to encourage environmentally and culturally appropriate modes of behaviour. Consciousness raising shall be strengthened by joint initiatives directed at the general public, including nation-wide, cross-industry campaigns. They must be promoted in every sphere of public life (schools, political parties and administrative agencies etc.).

9. Systematic Incorporation of Environmental Protection in Education and Training. Education and training equips those working in the tourism industry with the necessary skills for creating and managing environmentally appropriate tourism. A number of steps are required here: the development of special training schemes leading to recognised qualifications for environmentally sound management in tourism; the teaching of the required skills at all levels of training; the creation of training networks involving the small and medium-sized businesses; the sharing of teaching material; and the transfer of knowledge to customers, destinations and contractors. A start must be made not only al the level of vocational training and part-time courses and the respective institutions but also at universities and colleges that train senior tourism professionals. The proper training of tour guides and couriers is also especially important since they are important sources of information through direct contact with guests. Finally, international cooperation is also required in the sphere of education and training.

10. Establishing Evaluation and Monitoring. The process of restructuring to achieve sustainable tourism must be accompanied by the recording, assessing and continual monitoring of tourism-related impacts on the environment and of progress through the measures taken. Objectives and measures should be based on the results of the evaluation, i.e. on the systematic examination and assessment of environmental impacts. Consistent with this approach, the businesses and associations of the tourism industry as well as the tourism regions shall work together with the relevant government institutions to determine and analyse the ecological, economic, social and cultural consequences of their actions (e.g. by means of eco-audits and life-cycle analyses). Continuous reporting at national level (a "National Tourism Environment Report") would serve as an important instrument for assessing impacts and regularly reviewing progress in achieving sustainable development in tourism. At the company level, similar functions shall be performed by eco-audits or environmental reports, wherever possible combined with environmental management systems. The evaluation and monitoring must be based on meaningful indicators to be elaborated at national, regional and community level as well as in the companies sphere. Uniform criteria and standards are also required for giving consumers the balanced and sound information they need to be able to judge the environmental situation found in destination regions, in holiday facilities or in relation to the environmental impacts of package holidays on offer. Competitions and environmental criteria can be used as instruments to develop standards for environmentally appropriate management and local or regional development. This requires an ongoing exchange of data and information between all stakeholders, the harmonising of indicators and assessment criteria, and cooperation between the tourism industry and research institutions. The collection, processing, publication and general accessibility of environmental data on tourism (e.g. in the form of database, reports, data exchange agreements) should be supported. Advisory and supervisory committees must evaluate the results of this monitoring and consider what conclusions and recommendations are to be drawn from them. The undersigned associations and organisations agree to make these ten Guidelines the maxims of their action on the environment.

VI. Measures

The undersigned central associations and organisations of the tourism industry shall in the future intensify efforts to consolidate and coordinate their environmental activities. They shall first clarify how the necessary dialogue on this consolidation and coordination can best be organised. They shall thereby specify concrete measures to be implemented either jointly or under the auspices of individual associations. To this end, the tourism associations and organisations shall cooperate with government authorities, ministries, scientific institutions and environmentalist groups. The environmental declaration and measures are to be regularly reviewed and, where possible, developed further.

APPENDIX—V

DRAFT INTERNATIONAL GUIDELINES FOR SUSTAINABLE TOURISM

Comments on the Draft International Guidelines for activities related to sustainable tourism development in vulnerable terrestrial, marine and coastal ecosystems and habitats of major importance for biological diversity and protected areas, including fragile riparian and mountain ecosystems.

By Martina Backes, FernWeh-Tourism Review

We are grateful for sending us the International Guidelines for Sustainable Tourism and for the announcement and invitation to the Workshop in New Delhi. And we welcome the decision to postpone the workshop so that there is a modest chance to get property prepared. Not being aware or not having understood the scope of the Santo Domingo Workshop, we regret that we hardly shared experience or comments with NGOs from the South in preparation of the *elaboration of the International Guidelines*. Although a comment on background papers was posted by DANTE, the German Working Group on Sustainable Tourism to the yahoo e-group, we did not realise that the workshop might have been targeted at NGOs in general. We regret, we did not contribute much to make things more clear since we thought the workshop was planned particularly for offering appropriate opportunity to the South to realise participation and for giving more weight to the positions expressed by Southern NGOs. Although we welcome the CSD invitation to the CBD to participate in the international work *programme on sustainable tourism development* with regard to *biological diversity* and to *contribute to international guidelines*, we are "disappointed about the process which is utterly unclear and dubious. Our comment is twofold: First, there are some fundamental questions concerning the *preparatory process of the Draft International Guidelines* and second, there are essential points that we miss concerning its content In our view, the failure to mention important principles turns the Draft guidelines into a rather technical guidance tool instead of ensuring the necessary preconditions and some essential requirements that promise such technical approach to be successful, the Draft Guidelines remain silent about fundamental framing politics and about the conditions in which tourism actually evolves. Technical guidance alone will not be able to provide the means for sustainable tourism as long as counter acting political obligations are neglected. And, the more serious point, we doubt that the local-level stakeholders can claim any meaningful participation in the process of tourism management on the basis of these Guidelines. They might be involved, but they must not necessarily be involved when it comes to critical decision-making. So the Draft Guidelines do not sufficiently guarantee a frame for efficient involvement in final decision-making precesses communities and indigenous peoples.

A. The Process

It remains unclear how and by whom the Draft Guidelines were elaborated. Who worked out the workshop documents and who decided these papers, namely UNEP/CBD/WS-Tourism/2, to be the basis for further work? The authorship is not clear: who participated in the advisory and expert group established (by whom?) to come up with workshop documents? Second, the position and the level of participation of workshop participants is not dear, especially the difference between *'experts nominated by governments'* who *'attended'* the workshop on the one side, and representatives of International NGOs as *'observers'* on the other side. Did they all participate equitably and in the same way or did they have different levels of participation? Was the Workshop in Santo Domingo meant to be a regional preparatory event, occasionally followed by other workshops in other regions, in order to allow and ensure broad participation from the South and from local communities and indigenous peoples (as Michael Meyer had announced the search for workshop participants during the last general meeting of the *German speaking working group for sustainable tourism development in April 2001*)? Or was it meant to accelerate and to foster the process, leaving aside who will participate? Was the yahoo-group the only means of announcement and invitation, so that potential stakeholders awareness about the ongoing process was dependent on accidentally detecting the yahoo-group? Is that the way how the Secretariat understands multi-stakeholder processes to be generated? The open membership yahoo group, founded on 2 May 2001, offered the opportunity to comment on the workshop documents prior to the workshop. The Workshop report does not mention any position paper or comment from any interested stakeholder who did not participate in Santo Domingo but contributed by posting comments on the background papers in advance. The promise by the yahoo-group to *'collect all the comments and find a way of presenting them at the workshop in June'* in Santo Domingo' was confusing. The establishment of the e-group does surely not alleviate the shortage of time for reactions to the papers, nor the intransparent distribution of information by the Secretariat. Why is there no mention in the report?

B. The Guidelines

Guidelines without principles? We basically consider the elaboration of International Guidelines as a helpful step in realizing and complementing the work programme for sustainable tourism (CSD7). But we are worried about the Draft International Guidelines as there is no mention on any principles indispensable for sustainable tourism to evolve and for the security of local peoples' and local communities' livelihood, nor for the primary goal of poverty alleviation and equitable sharing of benefits. International Guidelines should at least mention the circumstances and describe the relevant existing realities and constraints that will be addressed. Usually international papers refer to underlying premises that need to be agreed upon and cannot be taken for granted-here the impact of tourism on social, economic, ecological and cultural aspects of biodiversity. We expected the guidelines to start with an underlying analysis, which does not only call for International guideline but gives more detailed reasons for its urgent need. Without designating the addressee the sender will fail to post the message. The analysis should include how existing tourism development hampers and affects biodiversity as the livelihood of the local people and the local communities. Although the Report on "Biological "Diversity and Tourism' JUNEP/CBD/COP/5/L.3) adopted by the COPS, mentions the impact of tourism on biological diversity and lists some aspects for the assessment of the '*interlinkages between tourism and biological diversity including benefits and economic importance*', the draft decision is non-committal and needs to be supplemented (find a comment on the COP 5 paper: www.iz3w.org/forum/deutsch). The guidelines offer the opportunity to supplement the COP5: Report with some fundamental understandings essential for sustainable development. The principles, that we expect to be mentioned and differentiated, include:

The primarily of the guidelines on tourism development an biodiversity should be to avoid dispossession and impoverishment: Under the contemporary political and economic conditions tourism is a major force for dispossession and impoverishment (economic, social, cultural and environmental). The draft guidelines mainly insfrumentalize tourism development as a tool for nature or ecosystem conservation, but who agreed that biodiversity needs tourism to exist? Poverty alleviation is listed jointly with several other goals, mostly conservation and economic development purposes, and one seems to be free to choose ("the *main visions and goals... can cover, inter* alia...). Instead of being listed under *"vision and goals"* poverty alleviation should be reconsidered in the guidelines. It should not be understood in the sense of the "poverty alleviation strategy" favoured by the World Bank. Who is to define poverty? The guidelines on tourism and biodiversity should not turn into a further pro-poor tourism initiative that simply aims to incorporate communities into free market system in the first place. In cases where poverty alleviation is defined by local people as a goal, it demands special strategies. These strategies need to be specified and their implementation needs to be prescribed, such as empowerment, people-centred development, and specific protection strategies. Just to mention the potential benefits that *'may take various forms including job creation, participation in tourism enterprises, direct investment opportunities* . (25) is misleading and ambiguous. Job creation alone does not guarantee livelihood security and income, as numerous case studies on tourism and local employment opportunities demonstrate.

The relationship between biodiversity and the livelihood of local communities and indigenous peoples: In the context of (tourism) development we consider biodiversity primarily as regards the livelihood of local people. The concept of livelihood includes cultural landscape diversity as a result of various land use methods. Furthermore, "livelihood" includes multifunctional services and capacities, including potential services, which help communities to be flexible and to react to various changes and socio-economic constraints. Tourism may provoke substantial changes in this system and may undermine these potentials of autonomous coping strategies, that are extremely important for people who live in marginalised area or for disadvantages people and communities.

Reference to subsistence and informal activities: In order to appropriately evaluate the impact of tourism on local communities' and indigenous peoples' livelihood and to assess the role tourism might play for local economies (by affecting control over and access to biological diversity and natural resources), subsistence economic activities and the level of self-determination and autonomy need to be respected. The guidelines hardly deal with the problem of suitable consideration of informal sector activities, which are usually not seized by statistic survey methods and which are difficult to record. Informal and subsistence or local market activities are extremely important for local communities to cope with marginalisation and economic crises or natural hazards. Tourism development that undermines peoples capacities of informal and subsistence activities may jeopardise the goal of poverty alleviation. How do the guidelines address this important issue?

Reference to the *"impact of tourism on the economy of indigenous and local communities, particular their, food and health security,..."*(81), as mentioned under 'monitoring", cannot really prevent adverse effects at this advanced stage of the management process. Reference should be made at an early stage and livelihood and local economies should be taken into account when gathering basic data and information prior to any decision.

The prevalent causes for contraproductive or harmful (tourism) development need to be specified: the politics with adverse effects (such as transport, employment, natural resource management, trade, services, patent regimes, climate) cannot be neglected and need to be referred to, and agreed upon. The responsibilities for these politics should not be ignored and need to be recognised and identified. At least, a consensus for the request to identify or to assess responsibilities and adverse politics should be part of the principles of the guidelines. In this sense, the international and national economic and financial settings, in which tourism evolves, need to be analysed in view of their impact on current tourism development. The rather strongly binding commitments WTO member stales have to follow require some special consideration, namely GATS, GATT and TRIPS. Leaving out these influential international agreements is ignorant and unacceptable, given that the liberalisation of services, the privatisation of collective use of biodiversity and the unfair competitive situation deeply affect the livelihood of local people and local communities and their access to and control over natural resources.

Only one actor- No responsibilities?

The Guidelines understanding of the multi-stakeholder process is doubtful: The draft guidelines address primarily governments as co-ordinators for a multi-stakeholder process. The understanding of "multi-stakeholder as a political goal led by the effort to correct unequal power relation, as we would like to see the approach, requires a different realisation. First, a deficiency analysis could identify those who are responsible for undesired and unsustainable developments. Second, a more participatory multi-stakeholder approach would identify those who need to be strengthened in their position (persons, agencies, organisations, bodies, enterprises). The actors at the different levels must be explicitly addressed by the guidelines, not to forget tourists and the private tourist sector. In a sound multi-stakeholder process responsibilities and duties are shared. The decision about who finally will be in charge of the co-ordination of the process should be left with the stakeholders.

Local level participation: for who's interests? The target should be to ensure balanced chances for all relevant stakeholders to participate. The authors of the Guidelines express their concern to get local stakeholders-in particular indigenous peoples and communities involved at (almost) each stage of the management process. But the way they answer to this concern stands for a rather distorted view of participation and multi-stakeholder processes. Although some support for local and indigenous communities in the field of capacity building and education was added to the management process (102-114), the repeated naming of local stakeholders in the draft paper can hardly be understood as serious approach to effective participation and involvement (24)." *Where local and community level visions and goals for tourism and biodiversity have been set, these may be taken into account by governments, when preparing the national level visions and goals....* (27)* Same to the next step, the finding of objectives: *"Where local- and community objectives for tourism have been set, these may be taken into account by governments when preparing national level objectives.'* (33). By co-ordinating the process of *"review of legislation and control measures it is important to involve and consult with all stakeholders. (27),* but it is not obligatory-so what? There is no clear indication that any community-level input must be taken into consideration when final decisions will be made on national strategies and plans or on a local level, i.e. when proposals for tourism development and activities at a particular location are to be approved or disapproved. *"Such decisions will be ultimately taken by governments..."(63).* So why should communities take the effort to prepare and present their own view, their own impact assessment survey and their wealth of traditional knowledge, if these inputs are not necessarily considered by government co-ordinators in their final decisions? Although governments are invited to consult all stakeholders who's input is an *important foundation of the decision-making process." (63),* this can hardly replace participatory decision-making. The interpretation of consequences that may derive from local inputs can still be drawn without their authors. The advantage for the tourist sector or foreign investors (i.e. external to the local community) is obvious: building on local knowledge and making use of their information becomes thinkable, although participation of local communities in final decision making processes is not principally binding. The COP5 Draft Report already acknowledges the importance of the knowledge of local people and communities and emphasises the important role, they play. But when it comes to criteria setting or to the defining of indicators and limits for carrying capacities- and this is the most relevant decision shaping instrument, local level involvement is not obligatory. Survey and control according to defined criteria may be implemented by locals, but then the standards may already be fixed without their involvement. Several times the importance of "consultation" of local level stakeholders is mentioned. This needs to be amplified by a more detailed understanding of what consultation, participation and involvement means, The proposal presented by Indigenous Peoples and Local Communities and NGOs on the CSD8 tries to specify the term prior informed participation. This paper could serve as a model for further definition. In addition, it seems problematic to address the local level stakeholders as a homogenous group. There is no attention drawn to disadvantaged people, nor gender aspects are considered. There is no difference between small scale local enterprises and the financially strong tourism sector from abroad.

Ignorance of stakeholders that shape the national and local level reality: How can the guidelines rely on governmental structures if taking into account the pressure of international debt policy, WTO agreements, private sector interests, employment policies or regional economic agreements (EU, NAFTA, etc.)? Those agreements broadly jeopardise the sustainable development goals, especially its social and ecological aspects. At least international development agencies and their decision makers, e.g. Northern governments, need to be clearly addressed, including World Bank and its Global Environmental Facility, IMF and Regional Development Banks. Further some clear responsibilities, requests and invitations to consider sustainable tourism and biodiversity issues must be defined for various international agreements. This includes UNCTAD, WTO-OMT, WTTC, UNESCO, UNEP, UNDP and CCCF (UN Framework for Climate Change Convention), Convention on Deserts and Convention on Woods (forthcoming). Some relevant working groups should be cited and addressed, and they should be invited to participate in the preparation of guidelines, i.e. ILO (to be cited as minimum requirement), Human Rights, WGIP, CBD Working Group on Article 8j, and CBD Working Programme of Indigenous Peoples adopted by COP 5.

Relation between local and community-level initiatives, small-sized enterprises and financially strong tourism companies: Finally the management process completely fails to pay attention to the disadvantaged small-sized enterprises. Local initiatives will face serious constraints to fulfil the conditions prescribed in the notification process. Community-based and community owned tourism projects are likely to fail as their plans and proposals for tourism development will have to compete with proposals form financially well-equipped tourism enterprises. Small initiatives presumably do not have the financial background to perform in concurrence with leading tourism companies. The capacity to produce all the papers and inputs requested for the notification process and later during the management process may decide on competing project proposals rather than their congruence with the goals of sustainable development. This is why the guidelines run the danger of boosting the unfair competitive circumstances of tourism development an thereby reducing the chance for sustainable community tourism. At worst, an increase in tourism in vulnerable regions will accelerate profit-making in the North while weakening the chances for local stakeholders to benefit form tourism, if not undermining their resource use and coping strategies.

C. Outlook

The preparatory process of the Guidelines is not transparent at all, but it is in line with the ambiguous process proceeding the UN-International Year of Ecotourism (who was invited to the preparatory workshop in Madrid and to the regional conferences? Who set the agenda?}. We finally see the urgent need to review and re-design the Draft Guidelines and to ensure due involvement and representation of local-level stakeholders in the preparatory process. It's incorrect to set the agenda first and to later ask a few randomly selected potential stakeholders to agree on predesigned goals under the pressure of time.

APPENDIX—VI

WTO ASIA-PACIFIC CONFERENCE ON SUSTAINABILITY CERTIFICATION OF TOURISM ACTIVITIES

Kuala Lumpur, Malaysia, 11-13 December 2003

Final Report

1. Background and Objectives

The need for greater sustainability in tourism services and activities is already widely recognized at all levels. Moreover, there are many and varied planning and development methodologies, as well as tourism management techniques that make it possible to attain higher levels of sustainability and to increase them gradually. Such methodologies and techniques can be complemented by voluntary certification systems for tourism services. The companies and organizations that provide them began appearing on the international tourism market in 1990 and have proliferated over the past few years.

Certifications and ecolabels basically serve three purposes, namely:

1) To stimulate tourism service providers to introduce improvements in their operations, aimed at greater environmental, economic, and social sustainability, by providing incentives and technical assistance to do so;
2) To differentiate and distinguish tourism products and services that meet environmental, social, and economic standards beyond the level required by the legislation in force;
3) To orient consumers with regard to the

sustainability characteristics of the tourism services available on the market.

Additionally, certifications and ecolabels serve to promote and stimulate higher levels of sustainability and quality throughout the tourism sector, aside from enhancing the image of certified companies, with the commercial benefits that such enhancement brings. Despite their recent proliferation, and partly because of it, certification systems have not managed to establish themselves among tourism enterprises in Asia or among tourists. There is also a lack of unanimity and homogeneity among the different systems that exist, resulting in confusion among users. As a result of its participation in various United Nations forums on sustainability, the World Tourism Organization embarked upon an analysis of the effectiveness of certifications and ecolabels in the different branches of tourism activity in 1999. The WTO published the results of this study in a publication released in 2002, and its Sustainable Development of Tourism Committee analysed these results at its third meeting, held in Costa Rica in September 2002. It also requested the General Secretariat of the WTO to prepare recommendations aimed at orienting governments in the field of certification for the purpose of setting up such systems, choosing from among existing ones, or supporting more widespread use of such systems. These recommendations were transmitted to the Member States in May 2003.

In this context, the Asia-Pacific Conference on Sustainability Certification of Tourism Activities was organized with the following objectives:

1) To disseminate the recommendations drawn up by the WTO on the subject of certification;

2) To foster permanent dialogue and cooperation among national tourism authorities, officials responsible for certification systems, and tourism service providers and their trade associations, to enable them to act in a coordinated manner in this area;
3) To move towards the harmonization of existing certification systems in Asia, at least in terms of basic procedures and criteria;
4) To contribute to the joint promotion of the concept and the practice of certification in tourism;
5) To consider the possibility of supporting a regional network of certifications and ecolabels for tourism sustainability in Asia;
6) To evaluate the advisability and need of establishing an accreditation system for certification bodies in tourism.

The Conference was convened by the World Tourism Organization, and hosted by the Ministry of Culture, Arts and Tourism of Malaysia. 107 participants from 12 countries in the region, as well as from international organizations took part in this Conference. Participants represented national tourism and environmental administrations, regional and local authorities, tourism trade associations and private companies, as well as NGOs and academic institutions.

2. Conference Programme

Thursday, 11 December 2003

9.30-9.45 Opening Remarks by Mr. Eugenio Yunis, Chief, Sustainable Development of Tourism, World Tourism Organization

9:45-10:30 Opening Address by Hon. Dato'Paduka Abdul Kadir Bin Haji Sheikh Fadzir, Minister of Culture, Arts and Tourism Malaysia

10:30 - 11:15 First Plenary Session: Introductory Presentations

·*Sustainability of Tourism and the Role of Certification*
Mr. Eugenio Yunis, Chief, Sustainable Development of Tourism, World Tourism Organization (PowerPoint Presentation)

An Introduction to Certification: A Tool to Support Voluntary Changes towards Sustainability
Mr. Ronald Sanabria, Director, Sustainable Tourism, Rainforest Alliance

Main Issues and Challenges about Certification
Ms. Alice Crabtree, Research Associate on Certification: Asia Pacific Region,
The International Ecotourism Society

11:15-11:30 Coffee break

11:30-13:00 Second Plenary Session: Case study Presentations of Certification Systems

An ICT Approach Towards Ecotourism Rating
Mr. Mohamed Daud, Professor in Knowledge Engineering, University Putra Malaysia, Selangor, Malaysia

Green Leaf Programme
Mr. Pradech Phayakvichien, Advisor, Tourism Authority of Thailand, Thailand
(PowerPoint Presentation)

Certification System for Sustainable Tourism in Nepal
Mr. Subash Nirola, Director, Tourism Products and Resources Development, Nepal Tourism Board, Nepal

VISIT - A Common Initiative of European Tourism Ecolabels

Mr. Naut Kusters, European Centre for Eco and Agro Tourism (ECEAT), The Netherlands (*Summary*) (PowerPoint Presentation)

Questions and Answers

13:00-14:30 Lunch

14:30 - 15:30 Third Plenary Session: Case study Presentations of Certification Systems

The Role of Certification Schemes in Tourism
Mr. Stan Rodgers, Principal Green Globe Trainer, AVTEQ Consulting Services, Australia, SHEMSI Sdn Bhd, Malaysia

Green Globe 21: A Global Sustainable Tourism Benchmarking and Certification Program for China's Tourism Industry
Dr. Zhuge Ren, Chief Representative, Green Globe 21 China
(PowerPoint Presentation).

Ecotourism Certification—Australia & Green Globe
Mr. Guy Chester, Director, EcoSustainAbility (Ecotourism Australia), Australia

Questions and Answers

15:30-15:45 Coffee break

15:45-18:00 Working Groups

Four parallel working groups debating on the topics of collaboration with other stakeholders, financing, facilitation of small and medium enterprises (SMEs), and marketing

20:00 Dinner hosted by Hon. Secretary General, Ministry of Culture, Arts and Tourism Malaysia at Bistro Saloma

Friday, 12 December 2003

Plenary Sessions to present conclusions of the working groups and to discuss on the following issues:

8:30-9:30 Certification financing

9:30-10:30 Recommendations to facilitate the access of SMEs and community organizations to certification

10:30-11:00 Coffee break

11:00-12:00 Certification and Marketing: Providing market advantage to companies and reaching out to consumers

12:00-13:00 Collaboration among governments, private sector and certifiers

13:00-14:30 Lunch

14:30-15:00 The Sustainable Tourism Stewardship Council and the Sustainable Tourism Certification Network of the Americas: Moving from Fragmentation to Consolidation
Mr. Ronald Sanabria, Director, Sustainable Tourism, Rainforest Alliance

15:00-16:00 Coordination of Certification Systems in the Asia-Pacific Region
(Plenary debate)

16:00-16:30 Coffee break

16:30-17:00 Closing Session

Closing remarks:

Mr. Eugenio Yunis, Chief, Sustainable Development of Tourism, World Tourism Organization

Representative of Ministry of Culture, Arts and Tourism Malaysia

3. Summary of Working Group Discussions and Plenary Debates

Problems, challenges, solutions and recommendations for certification were discussed in four working groups according to the following four themes:

1. The scope of certification - What should be certified?
2. Certification financing
3. Certification and Marketing
4. Collaboration among governments, private sector, NGOs, communities, academic institutions and certifiers

The working groups results were presented and further debated in plenary. The following list contains the main points resulting from the working groups and the plenary debate.

Theme 1: The scope of certification - What should be certified?

- Certification of products, businesses, guides, individuals, destinations
- Sustainability criteria and indicators (environmental, social, economic)

Problems, challenges:

- Which type of organization(s) should perform the certification and by which criteria?
- How to choose among the variety of certification offers in Asia-Pacific? Which one is really credible? - There is a lack of international standards and recognition behind them.
- Tourism products represent a huge variety of products and a large spectrum, which makes difficult to create common standards.
- The cost of certification can be relatively high for many companies.
- There can be various barriers for companies to entry.
- There is lack of incentives for companies to participate in certification.
- It is difficult to produce immediate benefits of certification.
- How to define the standards that are both specific to a region or country and internationally recognised at the same time?
- How to ensure that other players in the commercialization chain also conform to sustainability standards?

- International standards have specific challenges as developed and developing countries have different performance levels.
- What should be the government's involvement and role in certification?
- Market players have different levels of understanding about certification.
- Who should participate? How to involve local communities in setting up a certification system?
- How to define the target market of the certification program
- What should be the marketing level - domestic or international?
- Ensure enough benefits are attached to the program.
- The certification programme should be voluntary or mandatory?
- There is a need to provide training in the certification process.
- Convince industry to get onboard and maintain compliance with the requirements.
- Should certification be used as defacto regulation?
- Currently there are fragmented and isolated initiatives in the region, therefore there is a need for cooperation and networking.

Solutions, Recommendations

Scope of certification, what to certify:

- Certify the products and services as one company can run different kind of businesses.

- Destinations are also relevant to certify.
- Certification should be applied in a similar way for local businesses or international chains operating in a destination.
- Certification programmes could begin with hotels, but there is a need to consider the entire supply chain (life cycle) of tourism products, E.g. tour operators should ensure that the entire package (not just the hotels) be certified.
- Certification of guides can enhance the quality and professionalism in guiding services. Highly qualified and sensitized tour guides are especially important in fragile natural and cultural sites, and ethnic villages.
- Certified businesses should provide a code o. conduct to the tourists (e.g. on socio-cultural issues considering local communities), along with good information on the certified products and services that will foster responsible behaviour of consumers.

Criteria, standards and indicators:

- Development of criteria should be done through a bottom up approach with community involvement.
- In addition to the WTO recommendations for certification systems, it was suggested to include criteria in relation with:
    - Provision of proper wages for local employees
    - Harmony of the establishments with their surrounding

   - The need for the company to provide a code of conduct for tourists.
   - The consumers' point of view, such as safety and security, health, interpretation (tourist satisfaction).

- When consulting with communities it is also necessary to ask them to set up the maximum number of tourists that they are willing to receive at a time. This carrying capacity limit should be based on both cultural and environmental factors.
- Evaluate economic sustainability to ensure that tourism provides income for local communities instead of leaking to non-local investors. Include in the certification criteria how much of the economic benefits are redistributed among the local communities.
- There is a need to restructure traditional tourism indicators to reflect sustainability (e.g. tourism expenditure and how much of the benefits remains in the local communities).
- Set criteria and corresponding benefits for certified companies at different levels (the higher the level of criteria the bigger the benefit received).
- Include environmental issues into conventional quality schemes.
- It is necessary to define specialized standards for different tourism products and for countries or regions.
- Consider local culture in criteria of international labels.
- Create a minimum/basic regional standard for Asia-Pacific and define additional specific

standards considering the specific characteristics of the individual countries and their internal regions.

Development of certification systems:

- Make strong endorsement for certification as a definite value-adding element to tourism supply.
- Use sampling or pilot project to develop the program.
- Create incentives for companies.
- Offer certification services to those sites that are considered a priority from an environmental and social point of view. It is necessary that the certification programs proactively promote its services in such sites.
- Create/use an independent body to perform certification. If government is involved in certification processes, it should avoid political influence and rather play a facilitator and technical role.
- Government to play a role in providing incentives.
- Use hotels as pilot projects - e.g. use energy-saving as a theme to get started.
- Include both, process- and performance-based criteria.
- Use regional platforms and structures (such as ASEAN) to create certification systems & connect with international organizations to help create international recognition. Existing regional structures could be also used for benchmark and marketing.

- There is a need to create regional and sub regional alliances because there are differences in cultural and environmental matters. Standards should be established from the bottom, up to the local and then regional levels, building on the local/ regional realities, before they are brought to the international level.
- Provide training programs as part of the certification process.
- Start the certification process with self-declaration by parties to be certified as a step stone.
- Certification systems should sensitize entrepreneurs to develop a long-term sustainability perspective and considering the wider environment, instead of looking for short-term profits only.
- If used as de-facto regulation or policing of standards, the cost saved by government should be passed onto encouraging development of best practice and certification training and development.

Theme 2: Certification financing

- Financing of certification programmes
- Supporting of participating enterprises
- Facilitation of SMEs and community organizations to access certification (financial support and incentives, technical assistance)

Problems, challenges:

- Certification programmes should become self-sufficient in financial terms.

- How to avoid creating dependency on outside resources to cover the needs of SMEs?
- Political dimensions of financing: funding of certification systems should be such that it does not influence the neutrality of the certification process, i.e. should be independent.
- Social responsibility of governments.
- Access for SMEs and micro-enterprises does not mean just covering cost of certification procedure but also training requirements and implementation costs to meet certification criteria.

Solutions, Recommendations

Financing certification programmes:

- Aim at a mix of funding sources: governmental support, fees, donations, cash, in-kind
- Utilise various resources i.e. universities to guide hotels and other market players and to do research and help with monitoring to ensure continuation of conformity of the certified parties.
- Seek funds from international bodies, including international financial institutions (e.g. World Bank, regional development banks, such as the Asia Development Bank or Islamic Bank and other international organizations like WWF, IUCN, etc.).
- Governments to provide infrastructure support (e.g. secretariat - office, personnel, equipment).
- Government to provide seed money and create a revolving fund to cover basic operational costs.
- Engage tourism industry to finance certification

program (contribution from those who benefit, i.e. airlines).

- Working with voluntary services (volunteers).
- Co-operation to avoid duplication of efforts.
- Involve academic institutions and students for research projects.

Support of participating enterprises:

- There are financing needs for two main purposes:
    - for the process of applying for certification,
    - additional source of funding that help companies comply with certification criteria: capacity building and financing the technology that needs to be purchased to raise sustainability levels.
- Funding needs to be allocated for training with an emphasis on best practices but also include basic information on certification.
- Reinvest a percentage of tax from the tourism industry in local capacity development.
- Need to sell in innovative manner. Micro businesses will not buy into certification on the basis of saving the environment, but will adopt certification on the expectation of saving money (through implementing sustainable practices).
- Create incentives for certified products and companies, e.g.:

- tax reduction
- licensing advantages, longer permits

- better credit conditions (preferential interest rates, soft loans, state guarantee)
- government to channel funds through commercial banks by creating special credit packages
- marketing advantages with local and national tourism boards
- government grants, reimbursement of certification costs
- publicize awarding ceremonies,
- link awards for economical performance (e.g. best company of the year) with sustainability certification achievements.

- Reduce cost of auditing by concentrating high-rigor on-site assessment on products that potentially can have a high negative impact on nature and/or culture.
- Preferential access to funding is already often available to operators and communities that are indigenous people or located in protected areas. These funds could be considered also for certification purposes.
- In case companies internalize costs of sustainability improvements through a certification programme, it should be reflected in the price to the consumer. In order to increase willingness to pay by consumers, it is important to provide information for tourists on sustainability issues and certification.
- There can be a levy established on service prices and user fees, to finance sustainable management of areas and projects (e.g. in Nepal), but it is

important to explain clearly to tourists how that money is used.

SME support:

- Group companies for certification to bring the cost down.
- SMEs to form alliances for joint certification.
- Larger businesses support smaller ones.
- Create a foundation to support micro businesses.
- Undertake awareness raising and capacity building programmes especially designed for different types of SMEs.
- Create special financial packages for SMEs and local communities.

Theme 3: Certification and Marketing

- Providing market advantage to companies
- Reaching out to consumers

Problems, challenges:

- Create a package of incentives & benefits to market the programmes
- How to create a system that is recognised by the consumers?
- How the certification programme should be marketed?
- Multiplicity of logos confuses consumers
- How can the community help in the promotion and marketing of certification programmes?

Solutions, recommendations:

- Awareness raising on the benefits of certification, like improved company image
- Use relevant indicators that will help demonstrating the benefits of the programme, and thus promoting it.
- Develop regional cooperation to avoid proliferation of logos.
- Develop media support & publicity.
- Sell services locally.
- Marketing through tourism boards and trade missions (esp. overseas).
- Include information on certified products in official tourism promotion and information publications, as well as in websites and link websites of certified companies to them. For example, in Fiji, the Tourism Board has agreed to use images of certified products in promotional materials.
- Give priority to certified companies to participate in international tourism fairs. For example, in Australia, the Australian Tourism Exchange will have a large booth area for certified products, with preferential access for small ecotourism businesses.
- Government agencies to use preferentially certified products and services for public functions (e.g. meetings, trips).
- Companies to include logo and information on their certified products in their promotional materials.
- Providing information to schools.
- Official endorsement by international

organizations, such as WTO, or others, that will help create recognition of the programme

- Create one global logo
- One global web site with all certified products
- Provide incentives to consumers using certified products, e.g. free bicycle or public transport.
- Reach out to consumers through the involvement of consumer associations.
- Ensure that communities participate in the development of the certification program, and then they can help also promoting it directly to tourists. Promotion can come through word of mouth, raise the community voice to promote certified companies and, by default, certification systems will get more clients.
- Business to business recognition (Companies managing certified product uses/buys other certified products and services).
- If there is a country that has a sufficient number of certified businesses, it is recommended to convene meetings with foreign tour operators for them to learn about certified products. (For example, WTO has been promoting this with the Tour Operators Initiative. Workshops were organized in Turkey, Dominican Republic where foreign tour operators and local providers were brought together to define how could sustainability principles be implemented.) This type of workshops could be used to promote existing certification programs, in order to convince tour operators to give preferential treatment to certified operations at destinations.

Theme 4: Collaboration among governments, private sector, NGOs, communities, academic institutions and certifiers

- Areas of collaboration
- Mechanisms of collaboration
- Communication and networking

Challenges:

- What kind of collaboration mechanism and institutional framework could be set up at the national level (national council, steering committee, forum)?
- Which organizations should participate, who should regulate the process, handle the funds?
- How to create a regional network for the Asia-Pacific, and how to link regional networks?

Solutions, Recommendations

- Create political will in government and clear policy for certification.
- The process should not be solely top-down. It is necessary to develop participatory processes with involvement of government, private sector, NGOs (international and local ones), academic institutions, experts, local communities.
- Include stakeholders from sectors other than tourism, not treating tourism in isolation, integrating with more global sustainable strategies (e.g. health, safety issues).
- Involve national standards and quality organizations.
- Coordinate at different levels (national-regional-local).

- Reach out to local communities through workshops, fora, awareness raising, training and capacity building programmes.
- Involve the local context in international certification systems, collaborate with traditional leaders.
- Create a regional network of certification programs for Asia-Pacific, similarly to the Network in the Americas and the VISIT programme in Europe. The network should serve for sharing information and experiences in the first place.
- Create partnerships for coordination, communication, cooperation and transparency.
- Collaborate on branding and marketing (public-private partnership).
- Partnership with educational institutes for awareness raising and training.
- Create networking and easy-access information sharing mechanisms (e.g. database of good practices, certified products and companies Internet based mechanisms).

GLOSSARY

Attraction - any visitor service or product which tourists would enjoy visiting or using. An attraction may not be an "attractor" but can still be an attraction. To be considered an attraction, a product must be: A. Findable (clearly located on maps and street addresses, and directions provided). If tourists can't find the facility, it is not a tourist attraction. B. Hours of operation clearly denoted in any and all promotional materials (if a tourist arrives only to find the attraction closed, it is not an attraction). Examples of attractions include everything from a theme park that attracts over a million visitors a year, to a produce stand by the side of the road.

Attractor - a significant tourist attraction, which compels visitation. The primary "must sees" in an area. The top reasons a tourist would choose to visit this area.

Benchmarking - the process of comparing performance and processes within an industry to assess relative position against either a set industry standard or against those who are "best in class" (Synergy, 2000).

Best Practice(s) - a term used to designate highest quality, excellence, or superior practices in a particular field by a tourism operator.

Business Travel - Travel for commercial, governmental or educational purposes with leisure as a secondary motivation.

Consumer Show - a product showcase for the general public. Differs from a "Trade Show" as a trade show generally targets industry professionals. Consumer Shows target the consumer. Often there is a charge to get into the show.

Convention and Visitors Bureau - These organizations are local tourism marketing organizations specializing in developing conventions, meetings, conferences and visitations to a city, county or region.

Country of Residence - consists of the country where she/he has lived for most of the past year (12 months), or for a shorter period if she/he intends to return within 12 months to live there.

Cultural tourism - travel for the purpose of learning about cultures or aspects of cultures (NEAP, 2000).

Day visitors - visitors who arrive and leave the same day for leisure, recreation and holidays, visiting friends and relatives, & business and professional.

Destination Marketing - Marketing a city, state, country, area or region to consumers and trade.

Destination Marketing Organization (DMO) - a company or other entity involved in the business of increasing tourism to a destination or improving its public image.

Ecotourism - "responsible travel to natural areas that conserves the environment and improves the welfare of local people," according to The International Ecotourism Society.

Familiarization Trip - a complimentary or reduced-rate travel program for travel agents, airline or rail employees or other travel buyers, designed to acquaint participants with specific destinations or suppliers and to stimulate the sale of travel. Familiarization tours, also called fam tours, are sometimes offered to journalists as research trips for the purpose of cultivating media coverage of specific travel products.

Foreign Independent Travel or Foreign Individual Travel (FIT) - an international pre-paid unescorted tour that includes several travel elements such as accommodations, rental cars and sightseeing. A FIT operator specialises in preparing FITs documents at the request of retail travel agents. FITs usually receive travel vouchers to present to on-site services as verification of pre-payment.

Geotourism (1998) - tourism that sustains or enhances the geographic character of the place being visited—its environment, culture, aesthetics, heritage, and the well-being of its residents

Gross lettings - this refers to all room lettings, i.e. both paid & complimentary listings are included

Group Tour and Group Leader - Group Tour - a travel agent type company which plans motor coach trips. Group Leader: A small, informal group, such as a church group, scout troop, or social group. Usually one person plans the activities for the group. Some travel shows target these planners such as GLAMER.

Hospitality - a general term used in travel & tourism describing the "hospitality industry"; Refers to the general greeting, welcoming, food service, etc

Hotel Package - a package offered by a hotel, sometimes consisting of no more than a room and breakfast; sometimes, especially at resort hotels, consisting of (ground) transportation, rooms, meals, sports facilities and other components.

Incentive Tour - a trip offered as a prize, usually by a company to stimulate employee sales or productivity.

Inquiry - a request for more information about an attraction or destination.

Itinerary - a travel schedule provided by a travel agent for his/her customer. A proposed or preliminary itinerary may be rather vague or specific. A final itinerary however provides all details (flight numbers, departure times, reservation confirmation numbers) and describes planned activities.

Joint venture - a form of strategic alliance or co-operative arrangement where ownership is shared and a separate enterprise formed. This may strengthen existing businesses through shared expertise, capital, removal of competition and creation of economies of scale. International tourism joint ventures between foreign organisations and local partners facilitate introduction of foreign products into local markets.

Jungle tourism - Jungle tours have become a major component of green tourism in tropical destinations. A jungle is a subclimax tropical forest consisting of a tangled growth of lianas, trees and scrub which may form an almost impenetrable barrier to the tourist. Jungle tours are a relatively recent phenomenon of Western international tourism.

Key-informant survey - This involves interviewing people who are likely to have some insight into a problem: operating managers; sales staff; managers; suppliers; and consultants.

Keying - A social convention by which social 'reality' is transformed and seen as something else, such as the presentation of a fight as mere horseplay. In tourism, a peculiar, inverted variety of keying is frequently employed: the 'as if' situation in which participants are induced to playfully make believe that presented settings, activities or events are 'real', when as tourists they may be well aware that such occurences are contrived.

Leisure tourist - Leisure tourists, in contrast with business travellers, travel for pleasure and thus are not under any obligations to frequent specific destinations or facilities. They tend to be price and fashion conscious, concentrate their touristic activities to specific (vacation) times, and are influenced by marketing and publicity. Leisure tourism is heavily influenced by living standards, discretionary income levels and vacation entitlements.

Length of stay - This refers to the period of time which people spend in a destination. Many definitions require that visitors to a destination stay at least 24 hours or overnight, and less than one year, to be considered a tourist. Destination areas often look for means to extend tourists' length of stay in order to increase positive economic impacts.

Maximum room nights - this is calculated based on the total room inventory for all gazetted hotels.

Nature tourism - travel to unspoiled places to experience and enjoy nature.

Occupancy rate A tourism business occupancy rate refers to the number of airline seats or the units of hotel room space sold. This demand is usually measured as a percentage of available seats or space occupied for a given period of time. It is calculated by dividing the number of occupied rooms/seats by the total number available for sale during the same period.

Outbound - Outbound tourism is defined as tourism involving residents of a country travelling to another country. Outbound tour operators offer package tours abroad. They either operate the tours themselves, or they commission the services of an inbound operator to handle local arrangements at the destination. The country from which the tourists originate is known as the generating market or country.

Package Tour - A saleable travel product offering an inclusive price with several travel elements that would otherwise be purchased separately. Usually has a predetermined price, length of time and features but can also offer options for separate purchase.

Paid lettings - this refers to room lettings that are paid for by hotel guests

Quality - In tourism, the product is often intangible and quality is not apparent until after it is consumed. Quality has been defined as zero defects or defections, but still may be defined by the customer. The International Organisation for Standardisation defines quality as 'the totality of features and characteristics of a product or service that bear on its ability to satisfy stated or implied needs'. Others believe that quality is a combination of outcome and processes, including internal and external conditions, and is obtained when the expectations and needs of customers are met.

Rack Card - the typical tourism brochure sized 4" x 9" and used primarily in tourism racks. Also known as a "teaser."

Rack Rate - the official cost posted by a hotel, attraction or rental car, but not used by tour operators.

Resident - a person living in a given country, whether he is a national or not.

Sustainable tourism - this is, according to the World

Tourism Organisation, "envisaged as leading to management of all resources in such a way that economic, social and aesthetic needs can be fulfilled with maintaining cultural integrity, essential ecological processes, biological diversity, and life support systems."

Tourism - the business of providing and marketing services and facilities for pleasure travellers. Thus, the concept or tourism is of direct concern to governments, carriers, and the lodging, restaurant and entertainment industries and of indirect concern to virtually every industry and business in the world.

Tourist - temporary visitor staying at least twenty-four hours in the country visited for a purpose classified as either holiday (recreation, leisure, sport and visit to family, friends or relatives), business, official mission, convention, or health reasons.

Tourism Receipts - Tourism Receipts (TR) measures the total revenue received by Singapore from tourism activity. It includes all payments and prepayments for goods and services made by visitors, transit passengers, air & sea crew and foreign students (staying for one year or less) during their stay in Singapore. Visitors' payments to our national carriers (SIA & Silk Air) for international transport are also included.

Trade Show - a product showcase for a specific industry. Generally it is not open to the public. Differs from a "Consumer Show" in that a trade show targets the professional industry, while a consumer show targets consumers.

Travel Agent - the individual who sells travel services, issues tickets and provides other travel services to the travel services to the traveller sat the retail level.

Underdevelopment - Within development theory, the concept of underdevelopment suggests that wealthy capitalist countries have held back the development of so-called Third World countries. Tourism in Third World destinations is controlled for the economic benefit of foreign owners, reinforces dependency, lacks involvement of local decision makers, leads to negative sociocultural impacts, and results in the promotion of staged attractions to capture an international tourism market.

Urban recreation - the concept of urban recreation covers recreational activity that takes place in an urban environment in contrast to a rural setting. Participants in such activities are either urban residents themselves, day visitors from rural areas, or tourists. The major activities are shopping, visits to heritage sites, museums, movie theatres, operas, sport and music events, and indoor sports activities.

VFR - Visiting friends and relatives

Visitor - any person visiting a country other than that in which he has his usual place of residence for any reason other than following an occupation remunerated from within the country visited.

Visitors Centre - Travel information centre located at a destination to make it easier for visitors to plan their stay; often operated by a convention and visitors bureau, chamber of commerce or tourism promotion organisation.

World Tourism Organisation (WTO) - the World Tourism Organisation, a UN-related institution based in Madrid that collects data on tourism and lobbies on behalf of the industry.

World Travel and Tourism Council (WTTC) - The WTTC is made up of chief executives from all sectors of the tourism industry, including accommodation, catering, cruises, entertainment, recreation, transportation and travel-related services. Its central goal is to work with governments to realise the full economic impact of tourism. Its millennium vision is to make tourism a strategic economic and employment priority, to move towards open and competitive markets, to pursue sustainable development, and to eliminate barriers to growth.

Xenophobia - Xenophobia is an irrational fear or contempt of strangers or foreigners. This ancient cultural and political phenomenon is also present in contemporary tourism, mainly manifesting itself in the hostile attitudes of residents towards tourists. Xenophobia should be considered in domestic and international tourism in terms of economic, social and cultural distance, which is accentuated by the type and the number of tourists and the rate of tourism development.

BIBLIOGRAPHY

Airey, D. and Nightingale, M., 1981, Tourism occupations, career profile and knowledge, *Annals of Tourism Research,* 8(1)

Airey, D. and Tribe, J., 2000, Hospitality education, in C. Lashley and A. Morrison (eds.) *In Search of Hospitality: Theoretical Perspectives and Debates*, Oxford, Butterworth Heinemann

Airey, D., 1994, Education for tourism in Poland: The Phare programme, *Tourism Management,* 15(6), pp. 467-471

Airey, D., 1996, Tourism education and manpower development in Central and Eastern Europe, in G. Richards (ed.) *Tourism in Central and Eastern Europe: Educating for quality*, Tilberg, Tilberg University Press pp. 15-26

Amoah, V. and Baum, T., 1997, Tourism education: policy vs. practice, *International Journal of Contemporary Hospitality Management*, 9(1): 5-12

Ankomah, P., and Larson, R. T., 2000, Education tourism: a strategy to sustainable tourism development in sub-Saharan Africa, *DPMN Bulletin*, 79(1), pp.19-24

Cater, E. 1995, "Environmental contradictions in sustainable tourism." *Geographical Jounal* 161(1): 21-28.

Cave, P., 1997, *Placements in Industry - Experience in the*

Lancashire Business School, London, The National Liaison Group for Higher Education in Tourism

Chandra, R., 2005, *Wildlife and Ecotourism,* New Delhi, Akanksha Publishing House.

Chandra, R., 2006, *Recent Trends in World Tourism,* Akanksha Publishing House.

Charles, K. R., 1992, Career orientation and industry perceptions of Caribbean hotel and tourism management students, *Social and Economic Studies* , 41(1), pp.1-19

Charles, K., 1997, Tourism education and training in the Caribbean: Preparing for the 21st century, *Progress in Tourism and Hospitality Research,* 3, 189-197.

Chen, K. and Groves, D., 1999, The importance of examining philosophical relationships between tourism and hospitality curricula, *International Journal of Contemporary Hospitality Management,* 11(1), 37-42

Chen, S.C., 1990, The outline of higher level education in tourism in China, *Revue de Tourisme,* 45(4), pp.24-27

Chernish, W. N. and Spivack, S. E., 1998, Assessing the need for mutual understanding: health education for tourism educators and tourism education for health educators, *Asia Pacific Journal of Tourism Research,* 3(1), pp.45-54

Chon, K.S. and Shin, H.J., Hospitality and tourism education in Korea, *Hospitality Education and Research Journal,* 13(3), 215-224

Christie-Mill, R., 1979, Tourism education: Its development and current status, *Journal of Hospitality Education,* 3(2)

Clarke, L., 1992, A strategic perspective on employment, education and training issues in the 1990s, in J. R. B.

Ritchie and D. E. Hawkins (eds.), *World Travel and Tourism Review,* Oxford, CAB

Comic, D. K., 1989, Tourism as a subject of philosophical reflection, *Revue de Tourisme,* 44(2)

Conlin, M. V., 1991, Credible higher education in tourism: a Caribbean example, *Tourism: building credibility for a credible industry. Proceedings of the Travel and Tourism Research Association twenty-second annual conference*, Hyatt Regency Hotel, Long Beach, California, June 9-13, pp. 227-232

Conroy, B., 1997, Quality in education and training for tourism, in E. Laws (ed.), *The ATTT Tourism Education Handbook,* London, Tourism Society

Cook, R.A. and Yale, L.J., 1994, In search of a common body of knowledge for introductory tourism courses, *Hospitality and Tourism Educator*, 6(2), 39-42

Cooper, C. and Shepherd, R., 1997, The Relationship Between Tourism Education and the Tourism Industry: Implications for Tourism Education, *Tourism Recreation Research*, 22(1), 34-47

Cooper, C. and Westlake, J., 1989, Tourism teaching into the 1990s, *Tourism Management,* 10(1), 69-73

Cooper, C. Shepherd, R. and Westlake, J., 1994, *Tourism and Hospitality Education,* Guildford, University of Surrey

Cooper, C. Shepherd, R. and Westlake, J., 1996, *Educating the Educators: A Manual of Tourism and Hospitality Education,* Madrid, WTO

Cooper, C., 1993, An analysis of the relationship between industry and education in travel and tourism, *Teoros International,* 1(1)

Cooper, C., Scales, R. and Westlake, J., 1992, The anatomy of tourism and hospitality education in the UK, *Tourism Management,* 13(2), 234-242

Cooper, M., 1997, Tourism planning and education in Vietnam: a profile 1995-2010, *Pacific Tourism Review*, 1(1): 57-63

Cristureanu, C., 1996, The current state of tourism and tourism education in Romania, in G. Richards (ed.) *Tourism in Central and Eastern Europe: Educating for Quality*, Tilberg, Tilberg University Press pp. 75-92

Cross, J., 1998, Tourism education: the international dimension, *Tourism*, 97: 16-17

Csizmadia, L., 1998, Phare help in developing rural tourism education system, *Falusi Turizmus Tajekoztato*, 1(4), pp.12-15.

Cummings, L. E. and Brewer, K. P., 1996, Issues facing education in an emerging aspect of tourism: the gaming industry, *Tourism Recreation Research*, 21(2), pp.63-68

Daurer, C., 2001, Qualification in tourism - a challenge for education and training, *Tourism and Hospitality Management*, 6(1/2), pp.1-12.

Dayal, S., 2006, *Handbook of Tourism Ethics,* New Delhi, Akanksha Publishing House.

Echtner, C and Jamal, T., 1997, The disciplinary dilemma of tourism studies, *Annals of Tourism Research,* 24(4)

Echtner, C., 1994, Entrepreneurial training in developing countries, *Annals of Tourism Research*, 22(1):119-134

Ellias, S., 1992, The future of tourism and hospitality management courses, *Tourism Management,* 13(1)

Enghagen, L.K., 1990, Ethics in hospitality and tourism

education: A survey, *Hospitality Research Journal*, 14(2): 113-118

Enghagen, L.K., 1990, Teaching ethics in hospitality and tourism education, *Hospitality Research Journal*, 14(2): 467-474

Fayos-Sola, E., 1997, *An introduction to TEDQUAL: a methodology for quality in tourism education and training*, Madrid, WTO.

Fennell, D., and Nilson, R., 1998, The development of human resources through ecotourism, *Tourism Recreation Research*, 23(1): 82-84

Fletcher, J. and Latham, J., 1989, International tourism training, *Tourism Management,* 10(2)

Formica, S., 1997, The development of hospitality and tourism education in Italy, *Journal of Hospitality and Tourism Education,* 9(3)

Fox, R., 1998, Hospitality management education and quality tourism, *Tourism and Hospitality Management*, 4(2), pp.331-339

Gamble, P. R., 1992, The educational challenge for hospitality and tourism studies, *Tourism Management,* 13(1)

Gee, C., 1980, Professionalisation and travel industry education, *The Journal of Hospitality Education,* 4(2)

Getz, D., 1994, Students' work experiences, perceptions and attitudes towards careers in hospitality and tourism: a longitudinal case study in Spey Valley, Scotland. *International Journal of Hospitality Management*. 13: 1, 25-37

Go, F., 1988, Globalization and Emerging Tourism Education Issues, paper delivered to, *Tourism Education Exchange, University of Westminster*

Godau, A., 1991, Developing tourism managers - the Friedrich List Hoschule in Dresden, *Tourism Management,* 12(3)

Golembski, G., 1991, The needs of a higher level education in tourism in post-communist countries of Middle-Eastern Europe (as illustrated by Poland), *Tourist Review*, No.1, 3-5

Grgona, J., 1997, Role and importance of tourism staff at the turn of the millennium, *Acta Turistica*, 9(1): 91-106

Groves, D., 1996, A framework for the analysis of leisure-based academic and certification programs in travel and tourism, *Hospitality and Tourism Educator*, 8(1): 54-56

Gunn, C., 1984, Tourism education: filling the void, *Tourism Management,* 5(2)

Gunn, C., 1992, The need for multi-disciplinary tourism education, *World Travel and Tourism Review*, 2: 265-271

Hall, C. M. and A. A. Lew, Eds. (1998). *Sustainable Tourism: A Geographical Perspective.* Harlow, Essex, England, Longman.

Hall, C. M., 1991, Tourism as the subject of post-graduate dissertations in Australia, *Annals of Tourism Research,* 18(1)

Hawes, B., 1988, *Education and the Tourism Industry: Meeting the Challenge Together,* London, English Tourist Board

Hawkins, D. and Hunt J., 1988, Travel and tourism professional education, *Hospitality and Tourism Educator,* 1(1)

Hawkins, D., and Goldblatt, J., 1995, Event management:

implications for tourism education, *Tourism Recreation Research*, 20(2): 42-45

Haywood, K.M. and Maki, K., 1992, A conceptual model of the education employment interface for the tourism industry, *World Travel and Tourism Review*, Vol.2, 237-248

Haywood, K.M., 1989, A radical proposal for hospitality and tourism education, *International Journal of Hospitality Management*, 8(4), 259-264

Hegarty, J.A., 1990, Ethics in tourism and hospitality education, *International Journal of Hospitality Management* 9(2): 106-109

Hobson, J., 1995, The development of hospitality and tourism education in Australia, *Hospitality and Tourism Educator*, 7(4): 25-29

Holloway, C., 1998, Learning and earning: reassessing the aims and purposes of a tourism degree, in G. Richards (ed.) *Developments in the European Tourism Curriculum*, Tilberg, ATLAS, pp. 7-18.

Holloway, J. C., 1993, Labour, Vocational Education and Training, in W. Pompl and P. Lavery (eds) *Tourism in Europe - Structures and Developments*, Oxford, CAB International

Hope, C. A. and Muhlemann, A. P., 1998, Total quality, human resource management and tourism, *Tourism Economics*, 4(4), pp. 367-386.

Howell, R. and Uysal, M., 1987, Tourism education for developing countries, *Tourism Management,* 8(1)

Howie, F., 1996, Skills, understanding and knowledge for sustainable tourism, in G. Richards (ed.) *Tourism in Central and Eastern Europe: Educating for Quality*, Tilberg, Tilberg University Press, pp. 183-206

Hunter-Jones, J., 1997, Developing a methodology to identify the content of disciplines in tourism, in E. Laws (ed), *The ATTT Tourism Education Handbook,* London, Tourism Society (61-62)

IUCN Commission on Education and Communication, 1992, *Educating for Sustainable Tourism*, Slovenia, University of Ljubljana

Jafari, J. and Aaser, D., 1988, Tourism as the subject of doctoral dissertations, *Annals of Tourism Research,* 15

Jafari, J. and Ritchie J. R. B., 1981, Towards a framework for tourism education, *Annals of Tourism Research,* 8(1)

Jafari, J., 1990, Research and scholarship: The basis of tourism education, *Journal of Tourism Studies,* 1(1): 33-41

Jafari, J., G. Wall (1994). "Sustainable tourism." *Annals of Tourism Research* 21(3): 667-669.

Jandala, C., 1997, Education as a quality factor of tourism, *Tourist Review*, 52(4): 18-21

Jaspers, G., 1987, International harmonization of tourism education, *Annals of Tourism Research*, 14(4)

Jithendran, K. J. and Baum, T., 2000, Human resources development and sustainability - the case of Indian tourism, *International Journal of Tourism Research*, 2(6), pp. 403-421.

Jolin, L., 1999, Higher education in tourism: new routes to consider, Revue de Recherche en Tourisme, 18(3), pp.58-61

Jung, B. and Mierzejewska, B., 1996, Tourism Education in Poland: an overview, in G. Richards (ed.) *Tourism in Central and Eastern Europe: Educating for quality*, Tilberg, Tilberg University Press pp. 57-68

Kaplan, A., 1982, A management approach to hospitality and tourism education, *International Journal of Hospitality Management,* 1(1)

Ketyer, E., 1982, Tourism education in formal education, *Conference Proceedings of TTRA,* Salt Lake City, University of Utah

Khwaja, H.S. and Bosselman, R.H., 1990, Cultural adjustment of international graduate students in American hospitality and tourism programs, *Hospitality Research Journal,* 14(2), pp. 75-82.

King, B., 1994, Tourism higher education in island microstates, *Tourism Management,* 15(4), pp. 267-272

King, B., 1996, A regional approach to tourism education and training in Oceana: progress and prospects, *Progress in Tourism and Hospitality Research,* 2(1): 87-101.

Kivela, J., 1997, Education and training of hotel and tourism managers in Croatia, *Turizam* 45(5/6), 107-124

Knutson, B. and Patton, M., 1992, How prepared am I to succeed in the hospitality industry?, *Hospitality and Tourism Educator,* 3(1)

Koh, K., 1994, Tourism education for the 1990s, *Annals of Tourism Research,* 21(3)

Koh, K., 1995, Designing the four-year tourism management curriculum: a marketing approach, *Journal of Travel Research,* Summer, pp. 68-72

Kusluvan, S. and Kusluvan, K, 2000, Perceptions and attitudes of undergraduate tourism students towards working in the tourism industry in Turkey, *Tourism Management,* 21:3, 251-269

Lavery, P., 1989, Education and training in tourism, in S. Witt & L. Moutinho, *Tourism Marketing and Management Handbook,* New York, Prentice Hall (119-122)

Lawson, M., 1974, *Teaching Tourism: Education and Training in Western Europe: A Comparative Study,* London, Tourism International Press

Leiper, N., 1981, Towards a cohesive curriculum in tourism: The case for a distinct discipline, *Annals of Tourism Research,* 7(1)

Leiper, N., 1990, Tourism systems: An interdisciplinary perspective, *Occasional Paper 2,* Palmerston, Massey University

Leslie, D, 1993, Higher education for hospitality and tourism: a European destination, *International Journal of Hospitality Management*, 12(1), pp. 101-107.

Lundberg, C., 1998, A prolegomen to course design in hospitality management: Fundamental considerations, *Journal of Hospitality and Tourism Education*, 10(2): 26-30

McIntosh, R. and Walther, C., 1981, Teaching tourism in 4-year degree program, *Annals of Tourism Research,* 7(1)

McIntosh, R. W., 1992, Early tourism education in the United States, *Journal of Tourism Studies,* 3(1), pp. 2-7

McIntosh, R., van Weenen, I. and Shafer, E., 1983, Tourism education, *Tourism Management*, 4(2), pp. 134-139.

McKercher. B., Williams. A. and Coghlan, I., 1995, Career progress of recent tourism graduates. *Tourism Management*. 16: 7, 541-545

Medlik, S., 1965, *Higher Education and Research in Tourism in Western Europe, Study Tour Report,* unpublished

Medlik, S., 1987, *University Studies in Tourism,* Suva, Tourism Council of the South Pacific

Messenger, S., 1991, The UK hospitality and tourism industry; an overview of the issues affecting the supply of education and training in the 1990s, in C. Cooper (ed.), *Progress in Tourism Recreation and Hospitality Management Vol. III,* London, Belhaven

Middleton, V. and Ladkin, A., 1996, *The Profile of Tourism Studies Degree Courses in the UK 1995/96,* London, The National Liaison Group for Higher Education in Tourism

Mistilis, N. and Daniele, R., 2000, Education and Australian government policy: delivering information technology outcomes for tourism businesses? *Information Technology and Tourism*, 3(1), pp.3-14.

Moscardo, G., 1997, Making mindful managers, *The Journal of Tourism Studies*, 8(1)

Murphy, P., 1992, Community partnerships: the need for mutual education, *World Travel and Tourism Review*, Vol.2, 273-281.

O'Halloran, R., 1991, Ethics in hospitality and tourism education: The new managers, *Hospitality and Tourism Educator,* 3(3): 33-37

Ogorelc, A., 1999, Higher Education in Tourism; an entrepreneurial approach, *Tourist Review*, 54(1):51-60

Parsons, D., 1987, Jobs in tourism, *Employment Gazette,* 95(7)

Parsons, D., 1991, The making of managers. Lessons from

an international review of tourism management education programmes, *Tourism Management,* 12(3)

Pauko, F., 1996, University level tourism education in Slovenia, in G. Richards (ed.) *Tourism in Central and Eastern Europe: Educating for quality*, Tilberg, Tilberg University Press pp. 103-112

Pearce, P., 1991, Locating tourism studies in the landscape of knowledge, *New Horizons Conference Proceedings,* Calgary, University of Calgary

Pearce, P., 1993, Defining tourism as a specialism; A justification and implications, *Teoros International,* 1(1)

Petroune, I. and Voskoboinikov, S., 1998, Globalisation, localisation and identity of tourism higher education: a Russian perspective, in G.

Pirjevec, B , 1990, 'Alternative' tourism education and training, *Acta Turistica,* 2(2), pp. 140-145.

Pizam, A., 1999, The state of travel and tourism human resources in Latin America, *Tourism Management,* 20(5), pp. 575-586.

Pollock, A. and Ritchie, J. R. B., 1990, Integrated strategy for tourism education/training, *Annals of Tourism Research,* 17(4)

Priestley, G. K., J. A. Edwards, et al., Eds. (1996). *Sustainable tourism? European experiences.* Wallingford, UK, CAB International.

Rakadjiyska, S.G., 1990, Tourism training and education in Bulgaria, *Annals of Tourism Research*, 17(1), 150-153

Richards, G. (ed.), 1996, *Tourism in Central and Eastern Europe: Educating for quality*, Tilberg, Tilberg University Press

Richards, G. (ed.), 1998, *Developments in the European Tourism Curriculum*, Tilberg, ATLAS.

Richards, G., 1997, ATLAS: a European network for tourism education and research, in E. Laws (ed.), *The ATTT Tourism Education Handbook,* London, Tourism Society

Richards, G., 1998, A European network for tourism education, *Tourism Management,* 19(1)

Ritchie, J. R. B., 1988, Alternative approaches to teaching tourism, paper presented to, *International Conference for Tourism Educators,* Guildford, University of Surrey

Ritchie, J. R. B., 1988, Tourism Education in Canada, paper presented to, *International Conference for Tourism Educators,* Guildford, University of Surrey

Ritchie, J. R. B., 1992, New horizons, new realities: Perspectives of the Tourism Educator, in J. Ritchie and D. Hawkins (eds.), *World Travel and Tourism Review,* Oxford, CAB

Roberts, C., 1995, *The Environmental Agenda: promoting sustainable practice*

Roehl, W. S., 1991, Geographic illiteracy and the travel and tourism educator, *Hospitality & Tourism Educator*, 3(3), pp. 14-16

Rogozinski, K., 1985, Tourism as a subject of research and integration of sciences, *Problemy Turystyki,* 4

Ross, G., 1993, Tourism and hospitality work interest and motivation among potential employers. *Hospitality Research Journal*. 16: 2, 17-28

Ross, G., 1997, Hospitality and tourism job applications and educational expectation, *International Journal of Contemporary Hospitality Management*, 9:124-127

Ruddy, J. (ed.), 1992, Education and human resource

development for the hospitality and tourism industry, *Education Forum Proceedings Direction 2000,* Hong Kong, Hong Kong Polytechnic

Ryan, C., 1997, Tourism: a mature subject discipline? *Pacific Tourism Review*, 1(1): 3-5

Samenfink, W., and Rutherford, D., 1996, Academic contributors to the "Hospitality and Tourism Educator" volume 1 number 1 to volume 7 number 3, *Hospitality and Tourism Educator*, 8(1): 25-29

Sharma, Sunil, 2005 *Hospitality and Tourism Management Strategies,* New Delhi, Akansha Publishing House.

Sharma, Sunil, 2005, *Managing Hotel and Tourism Operation,* New Delhi, Akansha Publishing House.

Sharma, Sunil, 2005, *Hospitality and Tourism Marketing,* New Delhi, Akansha Publishing House.

Shea, L. J., and Roberts, C., 1997, A shift in teaching paradigms: From pedagogy to andragogy, *Journal of Hospitality and Tourism Education,* 9(1): 33-36

Sheldon, P. J., 1989, Professionalism in Tourism and Hospitality, *Annals of Tourism Research,* 16, 492-503

Shepherd, R., 1997, The graduate tourism aptitude test (GTAT), in E. Laws (ed.), *The ATTT Tourism Education Handbook,* London, The Tourism Society

Singh, S., 1997, Developing human resources for the tourism industry with reference to India, *Tourism Management*, 18(5): 299-306

Sivan, A., Yan, L., and Kember, D., 1995, Peer assessment in hospitality and tourism, *Hospitality and Tourism Educator,* 7(4): 17-20

Smith, J., 1998, Their mission: to boldly go where no school geography department has gone before: to explore a

14-19 vocational tourism pathway, *Tourism,* 99: 14-15

Spears, D., Boger, C., and Gould, R., 1999, Collaborative web-based project on tourism and marketing, *Journal of Hospitality and Tourism Education*, 10(4): 38-41

Stear, L., 1989, Towards a comprehensive and integrated approach to tourism management education, in J. Blackwell and l. Stear (eds.), *Case Histories of Tourism and Hospitality,* Sydney, Australian International Magazine Services

Swarbrooke, J., 1994, The future of tourism education, *Insights,* D21-D28

Tao, H. and Chang, D., 1989, The development and construction of tourism personnel, *Strategic Studies of Tourism Economy and Development,* Beijing

Tourism Training Australia, 1999, *Tourism and Hospitality Training Resources*, Sydney, TTA

Tribe, J., 1995, Tourism economics: Life after death? *Tourism Economics,* 1(4), pp. 329-340

Tribe, J., 1997, The indiscipline of tourism, *Annals of Tourism Research,* 24(3), pp. 638-657

Tribe, J., 1998, Community and commercial interests in tourism: Whose world is it anyway?, in G. Richards (ed.) *Developments in the European Tourism Curriculum*, Tilberg, ATLAS, pp. 19-30

Umbreit, T., 1987, The role of education in the tourist industry, *Conference Proceedings of TTRA,* Salt Lake City, University of Utah

Vukoniæ, B., 1996, Tourism Education in Croatia, in G. Richards (ed.) *Tourism in Central and Eastern Europe: Educating for Quality*, Tilberg, Tilberg University Press.

Vukonic, B., 1995, Tourism as a field of research and

Vukonic, B., 1995, Tourism as a field of research and education at the faculty of Economics in Zagreb, *Acta Turistica*, 7(1): 3-22

Walle, A.H., 1997, Hospitality and tourism education: Generic vs. specialised perspectives, *Journal of Hospitality and Tourism Education*, 9(1): 73-76

Walsh, M. E., 1992, Some recent innovations in tourism education in Ireland, *Tourism Management,* 13(1), pp. 130-133

Weiermair, K., 1995, Structural changes in the tourism industry and adaptation of professional training systems, *Espaces,* 133: 109-114

Westlake, J., 1992, Education for tourism: introduction, *Tourism Management*, 13(1),129

World Tourism Organisation, 1983, *Tourism and Employment, Enhancing the Status of Tourism Professions,* Madrid, WTO

World Tourism Organisation, 1987, *Education and Training for Tourism,* Madrid, WTO

World Tourism Organisation, 1992, *Repetoire Mondial des Institutions d'Education et de Formation Tourist,* Madrid, WTO

World Tourism Organization, 2000, *Tourism challenges in the 21st century: Human Resource Development in Asia and the Pacific,* Madrid, WTO.

Xiao HongGen, 2000, Tourism education in China: past and present, *Asia Pacific Journal of Tourism Research*, 4(2), pp.68-72

Xiao, HongGen, 2000, China's tourism education into the 21st century, *Annals of Tourism Research*, 27(4), pp.1053-1054

Yale, L. J. and Cooke, R. A., 1995, Content of tourism curricula: An industry delphi panel, *Proceedings of Research and Academic Papers,* USA, Society of Travel and Tourism Educators

Youell, R., 1997, GNVQs in leisure and tourism, in E. Laws (ed.), *The ATTT Tourism Education Handbook,* London, The Tourism Society

Zaccarelli, H., 1984, The development of an ethical strategy for managers of international hotels in third world countries, *FIU Hospitality Review,* 2(22): 1-11

INDEX

Y

■■■